IMAGE SEEKER

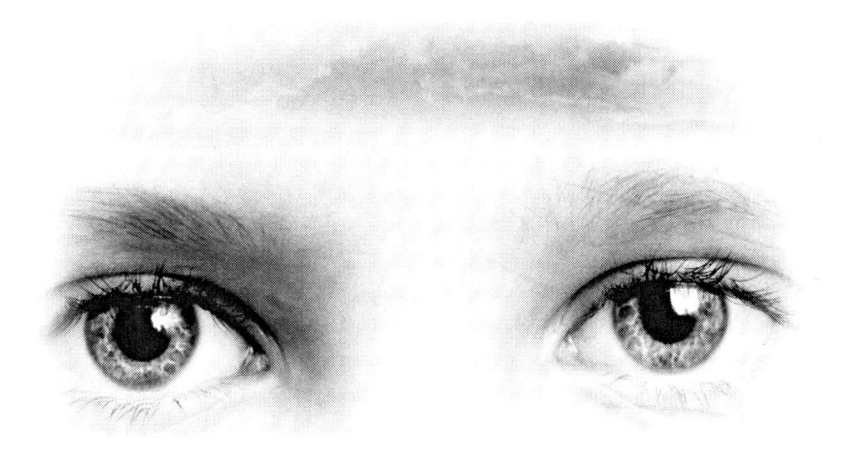

31 Daily Devotions for Those Who Desire to Look Like Christ

LuAnn Gerig Fulton

5 Fold Media
Visit us at www.5foldmedia.com

Image Seeker
Copyright © 2012 by LuAnn Gerig Fulton
Published by 5 Fold Media, LLC
www.5foldmedia.com

All rights reserved. No part of this book may be reproduced, stored in a retrieval system, or transmitted in any form or by any means-electronic, mechanical, photocopy, recording, or otherwise-without prior written permission of the copyright owner, except by a reviewer who wishes to quote brief passages in connection with a review for inclusion in a magazine, website, newspaper, podcast, or broadcast. 5 Fold Media does not capitalize the name of satan or any reference to the devil.

Scripture quotations are taken from the Holy Bible, New Living Translation, copyright 1996, 2004. Used by permission of Tyndale House Publishers, Inc., Wheaton, Illinois 60189. All rights reserved.

ISBN: 978-1-936578-26-9

Library of Congress Control Number: 2011944868

Dedication

This book is dedicated to my mom, Coyla Gerig, who taught me through her example to put Christ first in my life. Then, and only then, will I live, love, and serve to the fullest. Thanks, Mom, for showing me how to look more and more like Christ every day. May your legacy live on through me and may I, in turn, inspire others to seek His image.

For the Lord is the Spirit, and wherever the Spirit of the Lord is, there is freedom. So all of us who have had that veil removed can see and reflect the glory of the Lord. And the Lord — who is the Spirit — makes us more and more like him as we are changed into his glorious image.
  2 Corinthians 3:17-18

Special Thanks

To my sister, Marcia, a very special thank you for your editing of my book. Your help was invaluable and greatly appreciated.

To my children, Erica, Megan, and Adam, thank you so much for the privilege of being your mom. I know growing up in our home wasn't always easy with my health issues, but all of you stepped up to the plate and cared for me when I needed it. I am so proud of each of you, not just because you are my children, but also because you made the best decision in your life when you accepted Jesus as your Lord and Savior. My prayer is that you will always keep your focus on Him.

To John and Katie, thank you so much for joining our family and being the spouses that the Lord selected for Megan and Adam. I prayed for you from the time my babies were born and am so thankful that my prayers were answered with you. My desire is to be a mother-in-law that knows when to keep my mouth shut and one you will look forward to spending time with.

And to my husband, Dan, there are no words to describe how much you mean to me. You have been absolutely amazing throughout the years, never complaining about my health and all of its ramifications. You have supported me through all the good and bad times and even through all my hair-brain endeavors (even the writing of this book)! Many men would have given up on me a long time ago, but you believed in me and were the constant that I desperately needed. My prayer is that our love will continue to grow as we together serve our King of Kings and Lord of Lords!

Contents

Day 1	Image Seeker	9
Day 2	Summer Winter Blues	13
Day 3	Driver's Training	15
Day 4	Growing in Him	19
Day 5	First Day of School	23
Day 6	Nicknames	27
Day 7	The Fruit of the Spirit is Love	29
Day 8	Pain	33
Day 9	Lost Luggage	35
Day 10	The Fruit of the Spirit is Joy	37
Day 11	Hidden Behind the Door	41
Day 12	Pet Peeves	45
Day 13	The Fruit of the Spirit is Peace	49
Day 14	The Critter's Death	53
Day 15	A Quarter Call	55
Day 16	The Fruit of the Spirit is Patience	57
Day 17	Just Around the Corner	61
Day 18	Petal Pickin'	65
Day 19	The Fruit of the Spirit is Kindness And Goodness	67
Day 20	Back Surgery – Part 1	71
Day 21	Back Surgery – Part 2	73
Day 22	The Fruit of the Spirit is Faithfulness	77

Day 23	Letting Go	81
Day 24	I'm So Vain	85
Day 25	The Fruit of the Spirit is Gentleness	89
Day 26	I Stinketh!	93
Day 27	Full Custody	95
Day 28	The Fruit of the Spirit is Self-Control	99
Day 29	God's Sense of Humor	103
Day 30	Hyper What?	107
Day 31	He IS Coming Back!	111

Day 1
Image Seeker

So God created human beings in his own image. In the image of God he created them; male and female he created them (Genesis 1:27).

I want to begin this devotional book with a confession. I have not written this book because I have it all together and have life all figured out. In fact, you might as well know from the beginning that:

1. I do not have perfect kids.
2. I do not have a perfect husband.
3. My husband (unfortunately) does not have a perfect wife.
4. My marriage is not perfect.
5. My walk with Christ is not perfect.

Now I could lie to you and say that I have everything under control and I don't have any struggles, which gives me the assumed right to be an author. But the problem is that there are too many people who know me and are witnesses to the fact that it just isn't true.

Image Seeker

I have written this book for one simple reason: I care about you, plain and simple. I believe that Christ wants you and me to live a better life; a more fulfilled life—a life that looks more and more like Christ's life and less and less like the world.

Several things spurred me on to write this book. First of all, I started to wrestle with the fact that I was created in God's image. I began to really absorb the fact that my life, and yours, was so important to God that He gave the life of His Son for us. You and me, with all of our faults and problems, are His prized possessions.

That is sometimes hard to fathom, isn't it? When I look in the mirror, I have to be honest and say that I don't always think that I have been made in God's image because I don't often like what I see, either physically or spiritually. But when I really grasped the fact that I have been made in God's image, that my life was worth the life of His Son and that I am God's prized possession, my mind began to whirl.

Secondly, when my mom passed away in 2009, many people whom I hadn't seen in years came to the funeral home. I was so surprised when several of them told me that they couldn't believe how much I looked like my mom. They said they would have known me anywhere because I look so much like her.

And in turn, I cannot deny that two of my children are mine. Now I have three children, but my oldest, Erica, and my youngest, Adam, resemble me the most. Our middle child, Megan, is a mixture of my husband and me, but most people say that my oldest and my youngest look like me. Why do they look like me? Because they are my children, I gave birth to them, and they are a part of me.

Now you are probably wondering where in the world I am going with all of this. Well, all of these situations got me thinking that if I have really been made in God's image, if He is my father, shouldn't I look more and more like Him as I get older? If I see someone that I haven't seen for a while, shouldn't they think, *Wow, the older LuAnn gets, the more she looks like Christ?* When people are around me, if it is obvious who my earthly mother was, shouldn't it be obvious who my heavenly Father is?

As I have come in contact with more and more people, I have come to the realization that many of them are in the same situation that I found myself in several years ago. Yes, I had accepted Christ as my Savior, and I think I "looked like a child of God," but that's where it stopped. I had become stagnant in my walk with Christ and I wasn't becoming more and more like Him and looking more and more like Him every day.

Since then, I have recommitted myself to do all I can do to seek His image. I want to look more and more like Christ every day, and I am realizing that it can only occur if I understand that everything that happens to me is an opportunity to become more like Him. Writing this book has been a wonderful time to look back on my life and remember those opportunities in which I resembled Christ and then other times when I chose to look more like the world.

2 Corinthians 3:17-18 says, "For the Lord is the Spirit, and wherever the Spirit of the Lord is, there is freedom. So all of us who have had that veil removed can see and reflect the glory of the Lord. And the Lord—who is the Spirit—makes us more and more like him as we are changed into his glorious image."

These verses, along with the situations I just shared, have inspired me to be an "Image Seeker," and my prayer for you as you read these devotions is that you will want to be one too. This journey I am on is exciting and never dull, but it will be so much more fun if you join me! I hope that as I share my life with you on these pages, you will realize that every day you also have a choice—to use each circumstance to look more and more like your heavenly Father or to look more and more like the world.

Image Seeker

In some of the daily devotions, I will share with you something that has happened in my life that Christ has used (and continues to use) to mold and shape me. On other days, we will explore the attributes of the fruit of the Spirit because I have come to realize that there is no way we can look like Him unless these characteristics are alive and well in us.

Thank you for giving me your time to let me share these devotions with you. I don't take that lightly and I am humbled. As we spend this time together, please remember that today is a new day filled with opportunities to look more and more like Him as He changes us into His glorious image.

Image Seeker Prayer

Father, my prayer is that You will speak to us during the next thirty-one days. Challenge, stretch, and mold us into children who look like You. May those who meet us know by our actions and our words, that You are our heavenly Father!

Day 2
Summer Winter Blues

This is the day the Lord has made. We will rejoice and be glad in it (Psalm 118:24).

    I hate winter. Okay. I know…as a Christian maybe I shouldn't use the word "hate." So, I will rephrase my opinion. I really, really dislike winter. I can't stand to be cold. I don't like having to wear lots of layers of clothing just to feel one degree above frigid. I don't like snow, and I really dislike getting into a cold car and having my teeth chatter most of the way home. I hear people talking about their disappointment when we don't have a winter with heavy amounts of snow. Their idea of "fun" is to adorn themselves with long underwear, sweatshirts, pants, coats, gloves, mittens, socks, scarves, hats, shoes, and of course, the beloved ski mask. All of this is done so that they can journey outside and play in frozen precipitation. It just doesn't make any sense to me.

    So why am I not living in Hawaii? I have asked myself that question many times! But the answer I always come up with is that it is because God hasn't placed me in a tropical area; He has placed me in Indiana.

    But I must confess that because I live in the Midwest, I often have trouble expressing joy in the winter because of the frigid temperatures. Sadly, I have also found that if I'm not careful, it can rob me of my joy in the summer when it is absolutely gorgeous outside. How? Because on beautiful eighty degree days, I can find myself using my valuable time and energy in already beginning to dread winter. It is really easy for me to have my thoughts turn to the fact that someday these beautiful temperatures will be gone and I will have to endure yet another winter. So instead of thanking the Lord for the gorgeous day He is blessing me with and using my time to serve Him with my adoration and praise, I am already worrying about the cold, gray days ahead.

Matthew 6:34 reads, "So don't worry about tomorrow, for tomorrow will bring its own worries. Today's trouble is enough for today." Christ must have been thinking about me when He wrote these words, because He knew I needed this reminder. He is instructing me in this verse to not fall into the trap of wasting today, robbing myself of the joys of today, by worrying about tomorrow. I'm realizing that by my actions, I am telling Christ that I don't trust Him with my future; that my faith is not in the One that created me, but in my own humanness and frailty.

Will I ever learn to love winter? Probably not. But I'm working on praising the Lord for the many blessings He gives me today — whether the temperature is eighty or eighteen. So if you happen to see me on a cold, blustery day and I'm not smiling, you have my permission to scold me!

Image Seeker Prayer

Father, help me to remember that You made this day for me to worship and serve You. Impress on me that praise should always come out of my mouth, even if my teeth are chattering!

Day 3
Driver's Training

Follow my advice, my son; always treasure my commands (Proverbs 7:1).

Year: 1975. Location: California.
Emotion: FEAR!

I remember it well. Taking driver's training is often scary no matter where you live, but experiencing it in California with the freeways filled to capacity brought it to a whole new dimension. I went on my first day, fearful and trembling, just hoping that I would return home alive!

My first inclination that I was in for a memorable experience occurred when our instructor arrived. Remember that this was in the 70's and this man, who was supposed to keep us safe, looked more like he should be at Woodstock instead of teaching us to drive. Wild, unkempt hair, psychedelic clothing, long beaded necklace, flip-flops and a slow, laid back demeanor summed him up quite well. He entered the car eating fruit and proceeded to throw peelings out the window as we drove. Looking back, I'm sure this "hippie" looking man was very well qualified and probably a very nice person, but to this young girl who had been raised in a small Midwestern town, I was sure I would never see home again.

Image Seeker

Unfortunately, the situation only got worse. When it was time for one of the other students in our car to take her turn behind the wheel, I soon forgot about my fear of the instructor, who was now the least of my worries. She took her place behind the wheel and just sat there. After a few moments, the instructor asked her what she was waiting for and she calmly asked, "Where do I put the key?" Now if I had any brains at that point, I would have bolted while I still could, but I didn't. I looked at the young man sitting next to me in the back seat, and from the look on his face, I knew he wished he had made out his will before this trip.

She finally managed to get the key in the slot, turned on the ignition and we were on our way. But we soon realized it probably would have been better if the teacher hadn't told her where the key went, because she was driving down the left side of the road. After several moments, our instructor, in his relaxed way, calmly said, "Is there a reason why you are driving on the left side of the road?" Her answer was priceless. "Well, I just feel more comfortable on the left side."

My fellow hostage and I were frozen in fear in the back seat, having every ounce of blood drained from our faces. But once again, we heard our instructor calmly say, "Well, I feel more comfortable on the right side of the road, so please change lanes." She followed his orders and since you are reading these words, you know that I lived through the very frightening experience.

But you know what upset me the most? This girl received an "A" from the instructor. Granted, she did improve greatly and became a pretty decent driver, but I didn't think it was fair that she should receive a grade that high when she had put us through such an awful experience! I thought she should have paid a price for her past. But the teacher didn't care where she had begun; he only cared where she ended up.

I am so thankful that the Lord doesn't think like I do, because if my "grade" in life were to be determined by my past, I would be in serious trouble. Fortunately, He doesn't care about how bad

LuAnn Gerig Fulton

I was when I started, He only cares about where I am today and most importantly, the condition of my heart. What really amazes me is that if I have asked the Lord to forgive me of my past, He doesn't even have any memory of it.

What a blessing it is to know that the Lord already paid the price for me and is just waiting for me to obey Him by following His patient instructions. It is up to us whether or not we choose to stay on the right side of the road!

Image Seeker Prayer

Father, thank You so much for not holding my past against me and loving me for whom I am today. You are the ultimate 'instructor' and my prayer is that my ears will be attentive to Your gentle directions, because I know as I listen to You, I will become more like You!

Day 4
Growing in Him

But the Holy Spirit produces this kind of fruit in our lives: love, joy, peace, patience, kindness, goodness, faithfulness, gentleness, self-control. There is no law against these things! (Galatians 5:22-23).

    I am including devotionals in this book on the fruit of the Spirit because I think it is a great place to start when we are looking into how we can begin to look more and more like Christ. Most of us care what we look like on the outside, don't we? We want to look younger and have fewer wrinkles, we want to shed those unwanted pounds, and we want to find that makeup that will do miraculous things. As I started studying the fruit of the Spirit, I began to wonder why I spend so much time making sure my outward appearance is the best it can be, but I'm not nearly as concerned about what my inside is like. And I'm beginning to think that if I spent more time making sure my inner qualities were what they should be, I might even be a nicer looking person on the outside.

    So it is important that we begin to find out what Christ wants us to look like on the inside. What qualities should we possess that will make us more like our Father in heaven? We read in

Image Seeker

Galatians 5:22-23, "But the Holy Spirit produces this kind of fruit in our lives: love, joy, peace, patience, kindness, goodness, faithfulness, gentleness, self-control. There is no law against these things!" Sounds good doesn't it? I want to possess each of these things, but I must confess I don't always display them in my life.

Before we delve into each attribute of the fruit of the Spirit, we need to notice that it says in this verse the *fruit* of the Spirit, not *fruits*. People often refer to them as the fruits, meaning that they are like gifts or talents and we can pick and choose which ones we possess. That's not what Christ is saying here. Each of us has different gifts or talents. For instance, some of you may love to teach young children. Not me. That's not my gift. Some of you may be great at being a waitress and serving lots of people. Not me. That's not my gift either. My customers would end up wearing most of their food! My sister loves to do repetitive jobs. She gets really excited about jobs where you do the same thing over and over and over. When we were working on the wedding invitations for our daughter's wedding, she found out that we were going to be tying a bow on each one. She said, "Now I want to do that job, so make sure and let me know when you need them done." I didn't have to think twice about that offer. I really do not like to do repetitive jobs. And although I think that is a talent, believe me, I don't possess it. And you know what? It's okay. It's okay that I am not gifted to teach children, or waitress, or do repetitive jobs, because I have gifts and talents that others may not possess.

But it is different when it comes to the fruit of the Spirit. As a Christian, I don't have a choice whether I am going to possess these qualities. Christ didn't give *me* love, goodness and faithfulness and then give *you* patience, joy and self-control. We are all meant to have *all* of these characteristics — love, joy, peace, patience, kindness, goodness, faithfulness, gentleness, and self-control. If you have accepted Jesus Christ as your Lord and

Savior, then you possess this fruit. The question is, are you and I displaying this fruit and allowing Christ to grow this within us?

Do you ever wonder why Paul, who wrote this verse, used the word *fruit* here to describe these characteristics? I wonder if it is because fruit grows. Some of you have just the onset of the first buds of fruit, barely noticeable in your life. For others, those buds have begun to blossom and are just starting to become fragrant. Those blossoms give way to the fruit and, over time, this fruit grows and develops to full maturity. The process takes time. That's important to remember. These things aren't gifts or talents; you don't wake up one morning with the gift of gentleness or the gift of self-control. They grow slowly over a lifetime.

Not only does fruit grow, but the kind of fruit which grows on the outside is evidence of the nature of the tree. Apples grow on apple trees; pear trees produce pears. And the fruit of the Spirit, which grows in your life, is an outgrowth of what's inside you. It's the new person, new life, and new nature growing within you, which then expresses itself in the kind of fruit that grows on the outside.

The hardest thing to grasp about the fruit of the Spirit is that if you really want to see the fruit grow in your own life, you have to expect the fertilizer. What do I mean by fertilizer? Have you ever heard people say, "Don't pray for patience, because that's when the trials will begin?" Well, that's the fertilizer factor. For these qualities and characteristics to grow in your life, you must expect that you will have to go through some difficult times. Let me explain. It's easy to love someone who is a lovely person. A person who is nice, pleasant, and easy-going—they are easy to love, and by loving them, we aren't learning anything. But if we ask Christ to teach us how to love, He just may allow someone to come into our life that isn't quite so nice and pleasant. They might be downright nasty, bitter, and cranky. They may even live right in your home or, heaven forbid, attend church with you. A person like that is who teaches us how to truly love.

Now you may be saying to yourself, *Well, I just won't pray for patience or ask Christ to teach me how to love.* Allow me to let you in on a little secret. Christ doesn't need you to pray for these things. He doesn't need your permission to work in your life to build the new creation. He already has it. If you have accepted Him as your Lord and Savior, you already asked Him to make you a new person and gave Him full authority to do what He saw fit. He will work in you, whether you pray for it or not. Just because you don't pray for these qualities, doesn't mean your life will be easy. As Christians, we need to expect the fertilizer, to understand what it is when it hits you, and to focus on the fact that these situations or trials are fertilizer that will help your fruit to grow and mature.

Maybe you are struggling in your relationship with Christ and you have never given Him complete control. About now, you may be thinking that it might be best to keep it that way now that you hear you have to grow fruit in your life if you become a Christian. I want to share with you, from my experience, that I'd rather spend my life facing each day walking with Christ than without Him. I have the assurance that there isn't anything that He will ask of me that He hasn't already experienced Himself, and He promises to guide me every step of the way. I was talking to a friend of mine one day who had just started chemo for breast cancer. She said, "LuAnn, I can't imagine going through this experience without Christ walking with me." I can guarantee you will never regret the decision to follow Christ!

Image Seeker Prayer

Father, I trust that as we study each attribute of the fruit of the Spirit, that we will allow You to grow each characteristic in us so we will look more and more like You. Help us to give You complete control of every aspect of our life!

Day 5
First Day of School

"For I know the plans I have for you," says the Lord, "they are plans for good and not for disaster, to give you a future and a hope" (Jeremiah 29:11).

I remember the year 1989 just like it was yesterday. Our firstborn child was heading off to kindergarten and excitement was in the air. Friends would often ask how I was handling this first milestone in the life of our daughter, and I would always reply that we were all ready. Erica was a very bright child who carried on wonderful conversations with adults at the age of two, so by five she was ready for the challenge — or so we thought.

The first day of school arrived and the movie camera was rolling. A day like this just had to be recorded so that we could relive the happy memories for years to come. My husband got into position to capture the moment on film as I walked Erica out to meet the big yellow school bus. As we neared the road, her precious little hand squeezed mine with all her might. I looked down, and her beautiful big eyes told the whole story — the reality of leaving home to enter the big world without her mom and dad was taking its toll.

Image Seeker

We approached the bus door and I gave a big smile and wave to the driver. I told Erica good-bye and helped her onto the bus so she could begin her years of education. Unfortunately, Erica had different plans. As I backed away, she jumped back off and ran to me, falling into my arms, crying uncontrollably. I'm not sure whose heart was hurting worse at that time — hers or mine — but I knew what I had to do. Once again, I put her back on the bus and once again, off she came. At that point, fighting back my own tears, I had to enlist the help of the bus driver. I placed Erica on the bus for the third time and the driver held onto her as she closed the door and drove off.

As hard as it was, I knew that day that I had to make Erica face the unknown. It would have been so much easier on me to let her stay home under my watchful eye. But I knew that what seemed easier for me on that day, wouldn't be the best thing for Erica's future. Part of starting school was learning that, just like a turtle, we will never make it very far in life unless we learn to stick out our necks!

As I think back to that day, I realize how often I react to the unknown just like Erica did many years ago. God wants us to step out of our comfort zones to grow and become more like Him, but we often "jump back off the bus," running for protection in His arms. Remember that He knows what is best for us and keeps making us face the unsettling circumstances for our own good.

We read in Zechariah 13:9, "I will bring that group through the fire and make them pure. I will refine them like silver and purify them like gold. They will call on my name, and I will answer them. I will say, 'These are my people,' and they will say, 'The Lord is our God.'" The refining process isn't always easy, but the final product is worth the heat.

Erica began that refining process many years ago when she had to face that first day of kindergarten. That infamous day was just the beginning of many situations throughout her life that

LuAnn Gerig Fulton

would mold and shape her into the wonderful young woman that she is today! I'm praying that we will learn from her example of what God can do in our lives if we just "stay on the bus!"

Image Seeker Prayer

Father, why am I often so fearful of the unknown, wanting to stay in Your arms instead of stepping out of my comfort zone? Help me to realize that even when You want me to "stick out my neck," You will never let go of my hand!

Day 6
Nicknames

Then he told me, "The God of our ancestors has chosen you to know his will and to see the Righteous One and hear him speak. For you are to be his witness, telling everyone what you have seen and heard. What are you waiting for? Get up and be baptized. Have your sins washed away by calling on the name of the Lord" (Acts 22:14-16).

Most girls have cute, girlie nicknames growing up—Princess, Punkin', Angel, etc. Of course, I was the exception. My nickname as a young girl wasn't cutesy or adoring, but I guess it was well deserved.

Believe it or not, my nickname, given to me by my brother (that explains a lot!), was Walter Cronkite. Now if you are young, you may not even know who Mr. Cronkite was or for that matter, what he did for a living. He was a very famous American broadcast journalist, best known as anchorman for The CBS Evening News for nineteen years (1962-1981). He was considered to be one of the most trusted men in America because of his professional experience and kindly demeanor.[1] If you wanted to know what was happening in the world, you listened to Mr. Cronkite.

---

1. Wikipedia contributors, "Walter Cronkite," Wikipedia, The Free Encyclopedia, http://en.wikipedia.org/w/index.php?title=Walter_Cronkite&oldid=464429725 (accessed December 19, 2011).

Image Seeker

So why in the world would a young girl be crowned with the name of a male newscaster? Because I loved to be the first one to tell the world any news that happened. If we were gone from home and something newsworthy occurred, I would run in the house as fast as I could when we got home to make sure I was first to tell the news. My brother and sister loved to try to beat me to the punch, to deflate my opportunity to spill the beans. It used to make me so mad when they would say, "There goes Walter again, blabbing everything she knows."

As with many other childhood experiences that I thought were so traumatic, I can now look back at those days and laugh. It was a very fitting nickname and I guess I deserved the teasing. I just wish the nickname had stuck with me as an adult. I wish someone would say today that I'm just like Walter Cronkite, wanting to be the first to spread the news of Jesus Christ to everyone with whom I come in contact.

This is an area of my life that God isn't done with me yet. I know He has called me to be a newscaster for Him, but I often let fear get in the way. What will people think of me? What if I say the wrong thing and people make fun of me? But when I think about all God has done for me, including sending His Son to die on a cross, I guess stepping out of my comfort zone to share this news with others isn't such a sacrifice. It is an honor that I should embrace to be able to "blab" everything I know to the world.

So, why not join me and become a newscaster for God? I think this world could really use some more "Walters" walking around!

Image Seeker Prayer

Father, give me the courage and the wisdom to tell everyone I see about Your amazing grace. Help me to be a witness to all people of what I have seen You do in my life!

Day 7
The Fruit of the Spirit is Love

Imitate God, therefore, in everything you do, because you are his dear children. Live a life filled with love, following the example of Christ. He loved us and offered himself as a sacrifice for us, a pleasing aroma to God (Ephesians 5:1-2).

I got to thinking one day about how I overuse the word *love* in my daily life. I love chocolate, I love pizza, I love sunny days, I love my dog and cat, I love my kids, I love my husband. Yes, I do love chocolate, but believe it or not, that doesn't compare to how much I love my husband and children, even though I use the same word for both. I think of my love for chocolate as a surface kind of love, but the love I feel for my family is a deep, much more intense kind of love. I would die for my husband, Dan, and for my kids, but I wouldn't give my life for chocolate. (I know it's hard to believe, though there are times in my life where that has been questionable!)

I think that is the kind of love that Christ is talking about as a fruit of the Spirit. And it is also the kind of love that, I'll be honest, I can't do on my own. With some people and with some circumstances, I just can't love without the Holy Spirit's help. It just isn't possible. Once I allow the Holy Spirit to impart His love into me, it becomes much easier for me to be able to love others the way Christ wants me to love.

I think it helps to understand how we are to love if we have our priorities straight. First of all, we need to love God first and foremost. He wants to establish a one-on-one relationship with us, and we are to love Him with our heart and soul. If we are really in love with God, we will have a natural desire to want to seek after Him and include Him in every part of our life. We will want to spend some type of regular quality time every day seeking after Him, His ways, and His wisdom. When Dan and I were dating, I couldn't wait to spend time with him. If I didn't get to see him or talk with him every day, I felt miserable. But why is it I can miss a day of reading God's Word and really seeking Him, and it doesn't seem to affect me? I think that is why Scripture refers to Jesus as the bridegroom and we are His bride. We are to have that kind of intense and passionate love for Him each and every day. Matthew 22:37-38 says, "You must love the Lord your God with all your heart, all your soul, and all your mind. This is the first and greatest commandment."

Secondly, we have to learn to love our own selves. This is an area that can easily get out of balance. Some people are at one end of the spectrum and are narcissists. They are only concerned about their own personal well-being, their own agendas, and they assume that the world totally revolves around them. You usually don't have to tell that person that they need to love themselves. They are doing that just fine, in their eyes. That's not what Christ wants. At the other end of the spectrum are people who take the verse about dying to one's self literally and work on annihilating their own personality and become a doormat for everyone to walk on. That's not healthy either. We have to find a happy medium.

Many people struggle with low self-esteem and with loving themselves. Maybe you have had a horrible past, and you just don't love yourself. Maybe you grew up in an abusive environment or are in a violent relationship now, where you have been verbally or physically abused and have been told that you are nothing. That makes it hard to love yourself, doesn't it? Christ can heal you from your past, and if you allow the Holy Spirit to work within you, you can begin to love yourself in a healthy way.

Have you ever noticed in Scripture that it says that we are to love our neighbor as ourselves? It doesn't say to love your neighbor more than yourself or less, you are to love your neighbor as yourself. And I don't think it is possible for us to truly love others until we see ourselves the way Christ sees us and we begin to love ourselves.

Then we are to love others, whether it is your family, friends or neighbors. John 13:34-35 says, "So now I am giving you a new commandment: Love each other. Just as I have loved you, you should love each other. Your love for one another will prove to the world that you are my disciples." John 15:12 reads, "This is my commandment: Love each other in the same way I have loved you." Unfortunately, He doesn't say here that we are to love one another as long as that person is nice to us. He goes on to say that we even have to love our enemies!

Matthew 5:44 says, "But I say, love your enemies! Pray for those who persecute you!" *Ouch!* I don't know about you, but I find this really hard to do. It's easy to say, but very difficult to put into practice. I think we need to understand that it is next to impossible to do on our own. This is when we really need to rely on the Holy Spirit to work in us and give us love for those people.

This kind of love is not a feeling—it is a response. If we only love based on our feelings and our emotions, we probably aren't going to love the way the Lord wants us to love. This kind of love is a response to our obedience to Christ. He tells us in I Corinthians 13:4-8 what love really is. He says, "Love is patient and kind. Love is not jealous or boastful or proud or rude. It does not demand its own way. It is not irritable, and it keeps no record of being wronged. It does not rejoice about injustice but rejoices whenever the truth wins out. Love never gives up, never loses faith, is always hopeful, and endures through every circumstance."

When we read those verses and we see the words *always* and *never*, it's overwhelming isn't it? Always trusts, always hopes, love never fails. That tells us that as human beings, there is no way we can love like that on our own. It isn't possible. This kind of love is a divine kind of love that only Christ can give us. It means that when we are faced with someone who we can't love on our own, we need to think about how Christ would react to this person and how He would treat him or her. We need to act in obedience to how He tells us to love and then we can respond the way He wants us to respond.

As I said, this kind of love is not a feeling, it is a response. What is amazing is that what frequently begins as a response of obedience to Christ, can often end as a feeling. As we obey Christ and allow Him to love people through us, the feeling of love for those people increases.

Image Seeker Prayer

Father, help me to see myself and others through Your eyes, so that I can love unconditionally. You didn't just talk about Your love for me, You demonstrated how much You love me by Your actions. Please show Your love through me with those that You bring my way so that they will see You!

Day 8
Pain

So we don't look at the troubles we can see now; rather, we fix our gaze on things that cannot be seen. For the things we see now will soon be gone, but the things we cannot see will last forever (2 Corinthians 4:18).

Pain. I don't know how you feel about it, but I have decided I don't like it. I came to this realization when I was recovering from bladder and rectal surgery and if I had to rank surgeries as to how much fun they were, I was convinced this one wasn't even on the chart.

Don't get me wrong. I wasn't stupid enough to think that the time of recovery was going to be a piece of cake, but I wasn't prepared for the amount of pain that I would experience. Not only did I have the fun of having a catheter put in and then taken out; then put back in and then taken out; and then put back in... okay, you get the picture; I had the realization that sitting was going to be impossible.

Three weeks after I was strapped into stirrups, it took approximately five minutes of sitting to make me sick to my stomach and dizzy due to the severity of the pain. I kept thinking

Image Seeker

that I must be a big wimp since I was not doing well at handling this shooting pain in my derriere. I mean, for Pete's sake, I had birthed three children in my life, pushing them out through what seemed like a very small canal, without the use of pain medication. But I think what made the difference was that after my "wonderful" hours of labor pain, I had a beautiful bundle in my arms to make it all worthwhile. After this surgery, there was no bouncing baby…just the good news that sneezing wouldn't cause me to leak a river, if you know what I mean!

This experience made me think about how sad life must be for a non-Christian. Life is not easy for any of us, but for someone who hasn't accepted Christ as their personal Lord and Savior, there is no wonderful "bundle" waiting for them when their time on earth is over. In fact, what is waiting for them is hell, where they will spend their eternity in utter anguish.

I don't know about you, but I know that any pain I go through in this life, whether physical, mental, or spiritual, will all be forgotten when I enter the wonderful eternity in heaven that awaits me as a child of the King. I am confident that it will be worth it all when I see Him. Whatever you are facing today, first make sure that you have asked Jesus into your heart. Then keep your eyes focused upward, for that glorious day when you are called "home" to spend eternity with your heavenly Father! Trust Him, it WILL be worth it all!

Image Seeker Prayer

Father, I know that You never promised me that life would be easy or free of pain and suffering. But You did promise that if I remain faithful to You, I will someday enjoy the place in heaven that You are preparing for me. Help me to keep my eyes on You here on earth, so that I will look into Your wonderful face in eternity.

Day 9
Lost Luggage

Don't store up treasures here on earth, where moths eat them and rust destroys them, and where thieves break in and steal. Store your treasures in heaven, where moths and rust cannot destroy, and thieves do not break in and steal. Wherever your treasure is, there the desires of your heart will also be (Matthew 6:19-21).

Several years ago, Dan and I had the privilege of vacationing in beautiful Hawaii. It was a wonderful trip, filled with happy memories. That is, until the final day…

We left our resort to head for the airport, but had several hours to kill before we had to check-in. We inquired at the resort as to where we could go for a couple of hours that would be safe for us to leave our luggage in the trunk of the rental car. We were told to go to the nearby mall because the parking lot was heavily patrolled by the local police.

Yes, you guessed it! When we returned to our car about an hour and a half later, our trunk was completely empty. All of our luggage, movie camera, and souvenirs were gone. The police were called and a report was made, but of course, none of our belongings were ever found.

Image Seeker

We returned the car to the rental office and rode in the shuttle to the airport. On our way there, a gentleman in the shuttle with us inquired as to what had happened to our luggage. After telling him the frustrating details, he got a puzzled look on his face. He then looked at me and asked how I could be so calm when we had just been violated in this way. He said that if he had lost his luggage, he would be hysterical, ranting and raving (especially since he kept his cigarettes in his suitcase).

This opened the door for me to share with him that what we had lost that day was just "stuff." They were only material possessions that could be replaced and nothing that was stolen was going to heaven or to hell; it had no eternal consequence. I'm not sure the gentleman really understood what I was saying, but I've always hoped that maybe a seed was planted in his mind that day.

It is so easy to let the stuff of life become a priority that we hold onto with a tight fist. We need to remind ourselves often that our possessions won't be making the trip to heaven with us when we die. The Lord won't ask us how much junk we accumulated. Let's not forget that the world is watching how we react to the daily frustrations of life. If we look like Christ, it will be evident to them that it is Him Whom we serve. Who knows? The seeds we plant just might grow into a beautiful garden someday.

Image Seeker Prayer

Father, if I really want to look like You, then I know I cannot hold onto the things of this world. Help me to loosen my grip on the stuff with no eternal value and hold fast to the treasures that will make me look more like You.

Day 10
The Fruit of the Spirit is Joy

The Lord is my strength and shield. I trust him with all my heart. He helps me, and my heart is filled with joy. I burst out in songs of thanksgiving (Psalm 28:7).

I would be a hypocrite if I led you to believe that what I am going to share with you on this attribute are things that I have completely conquered in my life—because I haven't. This characteristic is still growing in my life and so my study of this topic was just as much for me as it may be for you.

I have found that joy is distinct from happiness. If my joy is based on what happens to me, I'm probably not going to be very joyful. Having true joy is being happy even when things aren't going the way I want or expect them to go. But do you know what else I have realized? If everything in my life is running smoothly and falling right into place, not only am I not learning anything about joy—I don't even know if I have any.

Now I realize that we are all living in a time when many people seem to have lost their joy. Job loss and hard economic times are taking their toll and many families are in disarray. It's hard to have joy in our present circumstances. Life for many people right now is the pits! Regardless of how badly you are feeling right now, Christ can fully heal, deliver, and restore you if you are willing to work with Him in the healing process.

One of the things that God can fully restore in you is your joy in Him. Once your joy in Him is restored, this quality will begin to overtake your personality and His joy (not your joy), will begin to flow in you. I guarantee you, once Christ begins to release His joy into your system, you won't be able to help but feel it.

It says in Nehemiah that the joy of the Lord is your strength. Without God's joy operating in your life, things can begin to dry up. Nothing is ever fun anymore. Everything can start to become a chore and before you know it, you want to withdraw from others and life in general. Life becomes too serious, and we forget to enjoy each moment that we are given.

I am beginning to realize that I would have a lot more joy if I just stopped sweating the small stuff. I need to stop worrying about the people who don't like me, or the people who have more than I do, or who's doing what with whom. Why? Because worrying about these things robs me of my joy. Instead, I need to cherish the relationships I have with those in my life. I'm learning that I need to think about what God has blessed me with, and focus on doing something each day to improve myself mentally, physically, emotionally, and spiritually. Life is just too short to let it pass by.

It is so easy to get hung up on what we don't have. As Christians, we are to have joy in spite of our inadequacies. We are often robbed of true joy because of our feelings of inadequacy. So many people struggle with low self-esteem. We do not feel worthy because of our failures and mistakes. We need to be reminded that we have been made by our heavenly Father and that He delights in us. Psalm 67:1 says, "May God be merciful and bless us. May his face smile with favor on us." Zephaniah 3:17 reads, "For the Lord your God is living among you. He is a mighty savior. He will take delight in you with gladness. With his love, he will calm all your fears. He will rejoice over you with joyful songs." Our Father loves us, takes delight in us and, as this verse in Zephaniah says, He even rejoices over us with singing.

Also, as Christians, we are to have joy in spite of our circumstances. The Christian faith offers joy in the midst of happenings. When Christians don't find joy on account of their happenings, they can always find joy in spite of them. We are taught not merely to accept limitations, but to use them. We need to take what we have and make something out of it. We must learn to live in spite of our inadequacies and our circumstances if we are going to have true joy.

Did you know that Christ's joy is always available to us? It is our decision to accept it or not. We often tell people that "He has made me glad" but unfortunately, by our actions we are saying, "If He does what I want Him to do, He has made me glad." We are choosing to not have joy, because of our selfish wishes and desires and wanting our own will, not Christ's will.

I think it is going to be very difficult for us to look like Christ if we don't have joy! So the next time you are tempted to display jealousy or worry, or feel like being grumpy, stop, take a breath, and begin praising Christ. Just as it says in Psalms, when our heart is filled with joy, we should burst out in songs of thanksgiving!

Image Seeker Prayer

Father, forgive me for focusing on myself instead of You. May my lips shout for joy as I lift my praises to You!

Day 11
Hidden Behind the Door

Don't keep looking at my sins. Remove the stain of my guilt. Create in me a clean heart, O God. Renew a loyal spirit within me. Do not banish me from your presence, and don't take your Holy Spirit from me. Restore to me the joy of your salvation, and make me willing to obey you (Psalm 51:9-12).

We remodeled our home when our son, Adam, was four years old. Walls were coming down, rooms were being destroyed, and our young son was in seventh heaven. He would get up each morning, strap on his own tool belt, and follow the contractors around throughout the day. Nothing made him happier than when one of them would ask him to help with part of the project. I'll never forget the day that they asked him to help tear out a wall. They gave him a hammer to use and told him to pound away with all of his might. He was exuberant, watching pieces of drywall fall to the ground as he flailed away with his tool.

The problem was that we never told Adam that this was the only wall he was allowed to destroy. In his young mind, if it was okay to take down one wall, it must be okay to take down another, and several days later, we discovered several holes in the wall in the hallway. It didn't take a rocket scientist to figure out who had done this destruction so we immediately found our young contractor to have a talk with him. Once we explained to him that there were only certain walls that would need his expertise in destruction, he promised us that he would never remodel on his own again.

You can imagine then how upset we were when a couple of days later we discovered, to our horror, another hole in a wall. This time it wasn't in the hallway where it could easily be seen, but we found it behind Adam's door in his bedroom. I'm sure our blood pressure had an immediate spike and probably smoke could be seen coming out of our ears as we called out for "Adam Daniel" to come immediately (our kids always knew if their middle name was included, they better not walk to where we were—they better run)! We just couldn't believe that he could disobey us so blatantly. But our anger slowly dissolved, when he looked at us with his big blue eyes and said, "I made that hole before I made the ones in the hall."

As I reflect on this episode in our family, I wonder, since the first hole that Adam made was behind the door, if he really did know he wasn't supposed to redecorate his wall with a hammer. I have imagined what might have been going on is his young mind. Maybe he made the first hole in a place where it wouldn't be seen so easily and when he got away with that one, became bolder and thought he would see what happened if his artwork was more visible.

I also wonder if that scenario comes to my mind because of the times I have done just what Adam did. I've had moments when I was tempted to do something that I knew was wrong, and I've given in to that temptation just enough to see if there were any consequences. I lose my temper with my kids, snap at my husband, or gossip on the phone with a friend, but because it is behind the door of my home, I feel somewhat justified in my actions. But the more times that I let this happen, the easier it is for me to behave this way outside the confines of my home. At that point, I'm not only hurting those in my family, but I then cause destruction with those with whom I come in contact. Unfortunately, it's those hidden actions that often lead to more serious transgressions that end with even more sobering consequences. I need to remember that when any of my actions don't line up with God's Word, it doesn't matter whether anyone else finds out or not—my behavior can never be justified.

Adam is now grown and his interests have turned from construction work to business finance. When we look back at pictures of those times, I sometimes yearn for those innocent days. I'm so proud that he is my son and I love him for who he was back then and for who he is today. And fortunately, it's the same way with my Father in heaven. He has loved me throughout my past and continues to love me now even during the times that I try to hide my actions "behind the door." I am still under construction as my Father in heaven continues to chip away those things in me that are not pleasing to Him. It's the knowledge that He loves me that much that makes me want to keep my actions and thoughts pure and be the child that He deserves.

Image Seeker Prayer

Father, forgive me for the times in my life when my actions aren't ones that should be on display for others to see. Keep me mindful that how I act and react affects others and should never have to be "hidden behind the door!"

Day 12
Pet Peeves

So get rid of all the filth and evil in your lives, and humbly accept the word God has planted in your hearts, for it has the power to save your souls. But don't just listen to God's word. You must do what it says. Otherwise, you are only fooling yourselves. For if you listen to the word and don't obey, it is like glancing at your face in a mirror. You see yourself, walk away, and forget what you look like (James 1:21-23).

Do you have any pet peeves? You know those things that happen in life that really irritate you. One of mine is fast talkers on answering machines. If you call our business and get our answering machine, you will be told to leave a message. I state in the message that I would like for you to *slowly* state your name, address, and phone number and we'll get back to you as soon as we can. Do you know what most people do? They leave a message that goes something like this: "My name is Gavin Mcshinsky from the Greater Baptist Gethsemane Retirement Center at 14363 Pumpernickle Drive, Amboy, Ohio 46823 and phone number is 555-568-4386." And all that information is rattled off in record time. Whew! It drives me nuts! I want to call them back, *if* I could understand the phone number, and say, "Didn't you hear my message when I told you to state your info *slowly*?" I give callers instructions and they just don't listen!

My second pet peeve happens all the time in stores as I wait to check out. You've been there. You've seen it happen. You wait in a line for what seems like hours (okay, maybe that is a little exaggerated) and finally the person in front of you has their turn. They stand there completely relaxed, watching each of their items scanned and bagged. The cashier then tells them that they owe $64.18 and it is only at that time, that they begin to figure out how they will pay for it. They decide they want to write a check, but of course have no idea where they put their checkbook. All of their other belongings are put on the counter, in hopes that the checkbook will appear. Once it finally is found, you get to wait while they ask for a pen and painstakingly fill in the blanks.

I often wonder if it is a surprise to that shopper that he or she has to write a check to pay their bill. Do they honestly think that the store will just let them walk out without paying? Why doesn't the caller on the phone listen to my directions and why isn't the shopper in front of me prepared for what they know is coming?

But if I am honest, I could say the same thing about me. Christ has given me His instructions through His Word and wants to have conversations through prayer to prepare me for what is to come. But so much of the time I'm not listening; I'm not communicating with Him and as a result I'm not prepared for today, let alone my future. I'm like the shopper. I know that Christ wants me to grow in Him, have a more abundant Christian walk with Him and begin to look more and more like Him, but I'm not doing anything to prepare myself. Just like the shopper knows that they are eventually going to have to pay for the items in their cart, I have enough knowledge to know that at some point my life is going to end on this earth and I will face the Lord. At that point, He may ask me "Why weren't you prepared, LuAnn? You knew this was coming, but what did you do to make sure you were ready?"

It is so important that we make it a priority to read God's Word and communicate with Him through prayer. What do we do when we get a new gadget or appliance that we don't know how to operate? We read the manual. And here we have available to us the manual, written by the Creator of the universe, and we're often too busy to spend time every day reading it, so that we can learn and grow to be more like Him. No wonder our life often lacks peace!

Image Seeker Prayer

Thank You so much, Father, for giving me Your Word that I can read and absorb. Help me to make my time with You a priority each day and then give me the wisdom and courage to follow Your instructions.

Day 13
The Fruit of the Spirit is Peace

And this righteousness will bring peace. Yes, it will bring quietness and confidence forever (Isaiah 32:17).

It is difficult to conceive that any person who truly has experienced the unconditional and generous love and joy of Christ in their heart could feel anything other than deep and abiding peace. Peace seems the automatic outcome of a life filled with God's love and joy. Why is it, then, that many Christians still struggle to find peace in their day-to-day living?

The Bible is filled with verses that promise us peace from God. Psalm 29:11 says, "The Lord gives his people strength. The Lord blesses them with peace." John 14:27 reads, "I am leaving you with a gift—peace of mind and heart. And the peace I give is a gift the world cannot give. So don't be troubled or afraid." We read in I Corinthians 14:33a, "For God is not a God of disorder but of peace." I could go on and on. Many verses tell us that peace is available from God, so why do many of us not have it?

Well, one thing I think we need to realize is that we won't have the peace *of* God until we have peace *with* God. It is impossible to have His peace dwelling in a heart that has not confessed sin. Our relationship must be right with Him before we can claim the promises from Him. So the first thing we need to do if we want peace in our life is to make sure that we have confessed our sin to God and asked for His forgiveness. We will never have true peace until this is done.

Don't you just love it when you are worried about something and one of your well-meaning friends says, "Well just don't worry about it. Most things you worry about never happen, so just don't worry about it. You are getting yourself worked up over nothing." That's such a blessing when we hear that, isn't it? I know I just feel so much better when I receive those pearls of wisdom! The sad thing is that I've said that to friends and family many times. But if we are going to be honest, many of us do make mountains out of molehills, don't we? There are things in our life that we just have to be willing to let go of—things that just aren't worth our time or our energy. If our life consists of becoming upset over one little thing after another, we won't have much peace or joy.

John 14:1 says, "Do not let your hearts be troubled. Trust in God; trust also in me." Do you know what Christ was saying here? He was saying, "Stop it!" We can see from this verse that we can control the way we respond to those things that trouble us. We can choose peace or trouble. We can choose to stay calm or to calm down if we start becoming agitated. He doesn't say in the verse to try not to let your hearts be troubled or do your best to trust in Me. No, He says, "Do not let your hearts be troubled. Trust in God; trust also in me." He wouldn't have said this if it weren't possible.

Let me share something with you that I believe if we implement in our life, we will begin to make the right choices and will have His peace fill us. Philippians 4:6-7 says, "Don't worry about anything; instead, pray about everything. Tell God what you need, and thank him for all he has done. Then you will experience God's peace, which exceeds anything we can understand. His peace will guard your hearts and minds as you live in Christ Jesus."

Now I've read these verses many times, but I realized something when I was reading one day. I realized that I don't have any problem remembering to tell God what I need, but I am often lax in thanking Him for all He has done. And it came to me that day that maybe my time of prayer would be much more beneficial if I would make sure and thank Him first for all He has done, before I begin to tell Him what I need. Prayer should be a time of worship, of adoration, of realizing Who we are praying to and how big a God we serve. How often do we start our prayer time with our problems, telling Him how bad things are in our life and our family's lives? How often do we start out by telling Him what our will is for our life and what He should do about it? *Oh God, do you realize how bad things are for me? Everyone is against me and I don't think you realize how terrible my life is. I need a job now and You need to provide one. My kids are driving me crazy, Lord, and You need to get them under control!* No wonder we don't have peace. We rush right into whining about our problems and we forget that we are praying to the One who created us, the King of kings, the Lord of lords.

If we spent as much time worshipping Him as we did unloading on Him, I think our perspective might change, because through our time of worship, something happens. Our eyes come off of ourselves and we begin to focus on God. When we realize how awesome and powerful our God is and how much He loves us, many times those things that we thought were such tragedies in our lives begin to fade. We realize that there isn't anything in our life that is happening today that this powerful, magnificent God can't handle. And, through our time of worship, our hearts begin to be prepared and softened, learning to accept God's will.

Music is a great avenue to worship the Lord in our time of prayer. If I'm feeling unsettled, I will often sing songs or choruses that express what I am feeling. I will never forget getting ready to go to one of my first surgeries. We had to leave early in the morning to get to the hospital and I was nervous and feeling unsettled. We got in the car and as the radio came on, I couldn't believe what song was playing. It was a song about the wonderful peace that only God can give. As I heard the words to the song, peace filled my soul and with each surgery that has followed, I have sung those words in preparation and it has given me the peace that I needed.

The wonderful thing about spending time worshipping our Lord, is that by the time we get around to telling Him our petitions, our attitude starts to change. Instead of spending our time wondering what God can do for us, we just might pray about what we can do for God. When Scripture tells us to give our prayers and petitions with thanksgiving, that will just be a natural outpouring of love for Him and desire to serve Him with everything we have.

When we get to that point, I believe peace will come. When we realize Who the God we serve really is, when we have worshipped Him, when we have praised Him, when our eyes have become focused on Him and His will for our life, the peace that passes all understanding will reign.

Image Seeker Prayer

Father, today I will choose to praise Your name, to lift You up and to remember what an awesome God You are. You are capable of handling anything that comes my way, so I will rest in Your strength and power, and enjoy the peace that only You can give!

Day 14
The Critter's Death

Give all your worries and cares to God, for He cares about you(I Peter 5:7).

    I love animals. In fact, when I was growing up, I often thought I would someday be a veterinarian. There wasn't a critter that I came in contact with during my childhood that I didn't try to make a pet out of. To my mother's horror, I even tried to make a pet out of a dead bird. I put it in a cage and for several days attempted to stuff food down its throat. I'm not sure what I was trying to accomplish, but with the grit that only a child can have, I guess I was determined to bring it back to life.

    One of the furry live pets that I had was a hamster. Today, they give me the heebie-jeebies, but, as a child, I thought my rodent friend was wonderful. I cared for him as if he was my baby and loved him as much as a hamster could be loved. I never saw it as a member of the rat family, but as a beautiful creature that needed me to take care of it. Unfortunately, he became ill one day and I was devastated. I knew that at that point, caring for him was beyond my capabilities, so I went crying to my mom looking to her for help.

Image Seeker

My mom felt about hamsters then like I do today and wasn't real thrilled about having close contact with this varmint. I'm sure she was secretly somewhat thrilled that we might have one less mouse to deal with, but in her infinite wisdom and love for me, she used the experience to teach me a lesson that I have never forgotten. She immediately warmed up a cloth in the oven and wrapped my beloved pet in it to keep him warm. Then she bowed her head and prayed for him, that if at all possible, my hamster would be restored to health.

I wish I could tell you that he immediately jumped up and was restored to perfect health, but he wasn't. But what I took away from that experience was far more important than whether my hamster lived or died. In that moment, my mom taught me that God was concerned about every area of my life and if something was upsetting to me, He wanted me to share it with Him. She demonstrated to me that I should pray about every area of my life, whether large or small, and that He would be with me no matter what the outcome.

Is there an area of your life that you haven't prayed about because you feel it is too insignificant to trouble God with it? Go ahead, lay it on Him. I know He will have time to listen. Then share the experience with your children or grandchildren. You never know when they may have a hamster that needs tending to!

Image Seeker Prayer

Father, I know that there are world issues that seem so much more important than my day-to-day struggles. But I am so thankful that You don't rank problems in order of significance. Thank you for caring about every aspect of my life and for allowing me to bring every care to You.

Day 15
A Quarter Call

If you need wisdom, ask our generous God, and he will give it to you. He will not rebuke you for asking (James 1:5).

My sister was driving in sunny California one day when her young son inquired as to why there were quarters in the console of the car. She explained to him that in the event of an emergency, the quarters could be used to make a phone call (this was in the olden days before cell phones).

After giving it some deep thought, wrinkling his forehead while this new information sank in, my nephew held one of the quarters to his ear and innocently said, "Hello…Hello!" Our family has had many laughs since then over his interpretation of his mother's wisdom.

Do you ever wonder if God chuckles sometimes at our interpretation of the wisdom He shares with us in His Word? He has spelled out so clearly for us in the Bible how we should live, but if we do not take the time to read and study, it is so easy to misinterpret what He is trying to tell us. He wants us to ask questions and He loves to see us be inquisitive, yet how often do we wrinkle up our forehead and do our own thing anyway? When I think of my life, I have to wonder if maybe God isn't always laughing at my misinterpretation, but is saddened at my lack of understanding or desire to absorb His teachings.

My nephew made his comment out of shear innocence, and I sometimes long for such innocence in my life. I often let so many things complicate my life and get in the way of really knowing my wonderful heavenly Father and learning from His wisdom. I need to become as inquisitive as a child, asking more questions and diving into His Word to find the answers. I need to hunger for more knowledge and then be committed to use that knowledge to be more like Him in a world that needs to see Jesus.

The next time you pick up your cell phone to make a call, think of my nephew and the quarter. Then think of a new question that you can ask your heavenly Father as you study His Word. He is *so* anxious to give you the answers you are searching for! And don't forget, as we learn from our Father, we will begin to look more and more like Him.

Image Seeker Prayer

Father, thank You so much that You never tire of my questions and are so eager to share your wisdom with me. Help me to come to You innocently, but boldly, as I glean from Your infinite knowledge.

Day 16
The Fruit of the Spirit is Patience

Since God chose you to be the holy people he loves, you must clothe yourselves with tenderhearted mercy, kindness, humility, gentleness, and patience (Colossians 3:12).

The next attribute that we need to look at has to do with other people, our reaction to them, how we treat them, and how we respond to how they treat us. Yes, it's that nasty word called *patience* that we need to explore. I think if many of us were honest, we would admit that we wish this characteristic could be left off of the list!

We live in an instant society—instant cereal, instant coffee, instant tea, and instant potatoes. I often catch myself standing at the microwave, tapping my fingers because it isn't cooking fast enough. We don't want to wait on anything anymore! The problem is that most of the instant foods we consume are not as tasty as food cooked the old-fashioned way. But if "instant" is all we have ever consumed, we don't know what we are missing. If you have never eaten my mother-in law's homemade macaroni and cheese, then that stuff that comes out of a box might taste okay to you, because you don't know what you are missing.

Image Seeker

This can be so true with our spiritual life. How many of us have spent our entire life settling for an "instant" relationship with Jesus Christ? Instant Scripture, instant prayers, and instant answers are just a few of the actions we think will bring us closer to Him. We breathe a quick prayer in the morning, telling the Lord what we need from Him today and, if there is time, we may even recite John 3:16.

The sad thing about this scenario is that if this is all that we have ever known, we don't know what we are missing. David shares with us these words in Psalm 40: 1-3, "I waited patiently for the LORD to help me and he turned to me and heard my cry. He lifted me out of the pit of despair out of the mud and the mire. He set my feet on solid ground and steadied me as I walked along. He has given me a new song to sing, a hymn of praise to our God. Many will see what he has done and be amazed. They will put their trust in the LORD."

David is telling us that because he waited patiently for the Lord, he was rescued from his troubles and the Lord put a new song in his mouth. Could it be that the reason we are often so tired and burned out is because we are living an instant life?

For us to have patience, we need to realize that there is *someone* in control of this world and our life. We need to remember that God does work things together for good for those who love Him. Patience is really faith in action. Our waiting on God's timing, having faith in the fact that He is in control, will result in an answer that will bring glory and honor to Him.

But waiting on God's timing isn't always on our agenda, is it? Think about it. For most of us, our lives are insane, aren't they? Our schedules are crazy. We spend much of our time feeling like we are running around like chickens with our heads cut off.

We run here and there and if we still have kids at home, we are running them to school or to practice and then back home to quickly throw a meal on the table. Or better yet, we drive through the closest fast-food restaurant and everyone scarfs down their food on the way to the next appointment. And by the time our day ends, we are exhausted and cranky and we surely don't have any patience left. It is no wonder that so many people are burned out and stressed to the max. Unfortunately, we're teaching our children that this is the way we should live because "everyone is doing it." Forget quality family time! It's not happening in a lot of homes today and it scares me. We are living in an instant society, and we don't have a clue how to wait patiently for anything and especially how to wait patiently for the Lord.

With whom are we to be patient? Ephesians 4:2 says, "Always be humble and gentle. Be patient with each other, making allowance for each other's faults because of your love." I Thess. 5:14 reads, "Brothers and sisters, we urge you to warn those who are lazy. Encourage those who are timid. Take tender care of those who are weak. Be patient with everyone."

The next time we find ourselves struggling to display patience with those around us, maybe it will help if we remember how short our time here on earth is and how never-ending eternity will be. None of us know how long we will have, but if you look at the entire picture, each of us is here for just a short time. But eternity will go on forever. Our not allowing the Lord to work in His time may affect the eternal destination of those with whom you come in contact. Our reaction to everyday situations may turn someone toward Christ, or turn them away. Turning someone toward Christ will mean that that person will spend eternity with Him in heaven. Turning someone away from choosing Christ as their Savior by our attitude, actions, and impatience means they will spend eternity in hell. Sobering thought, isn't it?

Remember that true patience comes as a result of having a deep personal relationship with Christ. We do not dare settle for instant Christianity. We have to be willing to spend time praying, studying the Bible, and listening for His directions. Patience is one of the characteristics of Christ, so the closer we try to become like Him, the more patient we will become, and then the more we will look like Him. And who knows? We just might have a few less gray hairs as a result!

Image Seeker Prayer

Father, forgive me for living my life on my schedule, wanting everything to follow my timing. Slow me down, Lord, and help me not to settle for instant Christianity.

Day 17
Just Around the Corner

Then the way you live will always honor and please the Lord, and your lives will produce every kind of good fruit. All the while, you will grow as you learn to know God better and better. We also pray that you will be strengthened with all his glorious power so you will have all the endurance and patience you need. May you be filled with joy, always thanking the Father. He has enabled you to share in the inheritance that belongs to his people, who live in the light (Colossians 1:10-12).

Yesterday, I shared with you my thoughts on patience. This is probably the attribute that I struggle with the most. Oh, I want patience, but the problem is that I want it right now.

Many times, when I think of patience, I think of the story of how Dan and I met. Dan was in charge of finding a speaker for his church's revival services and my dad had come highly recommended. Dan contacted my dad and arrangements were made for him to speak, beginning on a Sunday morning and ending Wednesday evening.

My parents went on Sunday morning and I went to our church. When they walked in the door for lunch, my mom informed me that I was going to go with them that evening for the revival service. When I inquired as to why I had to go with them, she said that she had met the man for me and she wanted me to meet him too. Now I don't know what your experience has been, but at that point in my life, if my parents thought someone was right for me, I knew to run in the other direction! I told her that he was probably already married, but she assured me that she had checked him out during the service and reported that he didn't sit with any woman and he didn't have a wedding ring on (makes me wonder if she heard a word my dad preached that day).

To make a long story much shorter, I did go that evening (pretty much kicking and screaming) to meet this man that my mom thought was amazing. I hated to admit it, but he did seem to be nice, and I even returned Wednesday evening and talked with him again.

But that was where it ended. He didn't ask me out, didn't seem interested, and we both went our separate ways. But then, one evening six weeks later, our phone rang. My mom answered it and came running down the stairs of our home to inform me that the person on the phone was Dan Fulton. I just figured he had called to talk to my dad again, but mom quickly informed me that he had asked for me and she didn't care what night he asked me out for, I *was* going.

I went to the phone and sure enough, Dan asked me out for the same evening that I was supposed to be in charge of a college age Christmas party for our church. But with my mom standing there, giving me that "you better listen to me, child" look, I told him that I was free that evening and would love to go out with him.

The rest is history as they say. Our first date was in December, we were engaged in April, and married in October. That was thirty years ago and we are still going strong. My mom wasn't always right, but she sure knew what she was talking about in this particular instance.

LuAnn Gerig Fulton

So what in the world does this story have to do with patience? Well, the part of the story that I left out was that my husband is six-and-a-half years older than I am. When we married, I was twenty-one and he was twenty-eight and that has never been an issue in our marriage. But we often joke that if the Lord would have had us meet when Dan began praying for a wife at age twenty-one, I would have only been fifteen, and my mom would have seriously frowned on that relationship then!

Because Dan was patient and waited for the Lord to "grow up" his wife, he got me. Now, most days I think he is glad he waited, but I'm sure there are times he wonders why.

Our story makes me wonder how many blessings I miss out on in life because I lack patience. I wonder what is just around the corner that is fantastic, but because I don't wait on the Lord for *His* timing, I miss out. As I shared yesterday, for us to have patience, we need to realize that there is *someone* in control of this world and our life and remember that God does work things together for good for those who love Him. Remember, our waiting on God's timing, having faith in the fact that He is in control, will result in an answer that will bring glory and honor to Him.

Image Seeker Prayer

Father, help me to remember that You are in control and that You have perfect timing. Help me to put my trust in You and allow You to work your will in my life at just the right time.

Day 18
Petal Pickin'

See how very much our Father loves us, for he calls us his children, and that is what we are! But the people who belong to this world don't recognize that we are God's children because they don't know him (I John 3:1).

When I was a child, I can remember going through the scientific process of deciding whether a certain boy liked me or not. I would take a flower and begin pulling the petals off one by one, saying the familiar line, "He loves me, he loves me not." Of course if I managed to get to the last petal and the line was "He loves me," I was ecstatic and knew I had found true love. But if there was a tragic turn of events and the last petal spoke the truth that he didn't love me, I was devastated.

So, what would I do to avoid the possible tragic ending? I would cheat. Yes, it's time I confess my sin of cheating with flowers. If I counted ahead and saw that it would end with the life-shattering news that he didn't love me, I would only tear half of the next petal off, creating an extra petal to pull, ensuring a happy ending.

As an adult, I remember those days with a smile and a shake of the head, wondering how in the world I could have trusted the outcome of love to a flower. How could I have even entertained the thought that the positive result of "petal pickin'" would ensure the love of the boy for that particular week, day, or even hour?

But yet, as I examine my life today and talk with other people concerning their thoughts and feelings, I am realizing that we, as adults, often look at God's love for us in relatively the same way. Oh, we may not resort to petal pickin', but we often play the game of wondering if God really loves us the way we are, or if it is necessary to cheat and connive to get Him to really care about us.

As I have progressed in my Christian journey, I have come to the conclusion that I am loved by God just because I am me. He doesn't care about me because of anything great or wonderful that I have done in my past, or because of some amazing, deeply spiritual work that I may be doing today, or even because I may become a saint in the future. No, God loves me today because I am me and most importantly, I am His.

I am sharing my life with you on these pages with the hope that you will be reminded that whatever happens to you and me on this journey called "life" is in God's plan. Each situation is really a petal pickin' experience that will not determine whether we are loved by our Father, but will help mold us into who He wants us to be and help us to be more like Him. The more we allow our Father to love and shape us through all of the experiences that come our way, the less preoccupied we will be about which "petal" we will end up with.

Image Seeker Prayer

Father, thank You so much that Your love for me doesn't depend on the petals of a flower or on Your mood for the day. Help me Lord to feel Your love in a new and powerful way today as I thank You for making me the person that You have created in Your image.

Day 19
The Fruit of the Spirit is Kindness and Goodness

Since God chose you to be the holy people he loves, you must clothe yourselves with tenderhearted mercy, kindness, humility, gentleness, and patience (Colossians 3:12).

We are going to look at the next two attributes of the fruit of the Spirit at the same time, because I believe they go hand in hand. They are kindness and goodness. Now, if you struggle with having patience, it can be a struggle to study kindness and goodness. It is hard to display kindness and goodness when your patience is low and you feel like biting people's heads off (not that I would know anything about that).

When you look at these two words, it is easy to think of them as the easy fruit to have. We all like to think of ourselves as kind and good people, and so to think otherwise is hard to swallow. And if I'm really honest, I realize that I have a long way to go to have the kindness and goodness that Christ wants me to have.

Proverbs 12:25 says, "Worry weighs a person down; an encouraging word cheers a person up." We read in Proverbs 14:31, "Those who oppress the poor insult their Maker, but helping the poor honors him." 2 Timothy 2:24 reads, "A servant of the Lord must not quarrel but must be kind to everyone, be able to teach, and be patient with difficult people."

And I could go on and on listing verses that tell us to be kind — not just to people we love, but to everyone that we meet. Let's be honest, sometimes it's easier to be kind to complete strangers than it is to be kind to those that we love. When my kids were younger, they often caught me at that. I would go from yelling at them to answering our business phone, and my level of kindness changed dramatically! "YOU GET OVER HERE RIGHT NOW! DID YOU HEAR ME?" and then the business line would ring and I'd answer, "Good afternoon, Dan's Fish Fry" in a very pleasant voice. Now, before you think of me so piously, what happens inside your car on the way to church Sunday mornings? How many of you have been yelling at each other on the way to church and then you all get out of the car and walk into church looking like you have the joy of the Lord? It's tough to show kindness sometimes, isn't it?

Christ, of course, never asks us to have a quality that He didn't have and Christ is the true example of kindness. In Titus 3:4-8 are these words, "When God our Savior revealed his kindness and love, he saved us, not because of the righteous things we had done, but because of his mercy. He washed away our sins, giving us a new birth and new life through the Holy Spirit. He generously poured out the Spirit upon us through Jesus Christ our Savior. Because of his grace he declared us righteous and gave us confidence that we will inherit eternal life. This is a trustworthy saying, and I want you to insist on these teachings so that all who trust in God will devote themselves to doing good. These teachings are good and beneficial for everyone."

I do not deserve kindness from God, but He freely gives it to me anyway because He loves me so much. If Christ is my example, then I have to ask myself if that is the type of kindness that I have. Do I love others enough to show them kindness, even if at times, they don't deserve it? I've had to search myself to see if when I am kind to people, is it a result of the goodness in my life or is it because I think I'll get something in return if I am kind? In other words, am I a phony? Do I genuinely care about others and do I love them unconditionally?

    I have met people who seemed really kind on the outside, but their life proved they were rotten to the core once I got to know them. They are like a beautifully wrapped gift. Imagine that you are given a gift and the outside is exquisite in looks—beautiful wrapping paper and a gorgeous matching bow. It's so pretty that you almost hate to tear the paper to open it up, but you figure what's inside must be wonderful since the outside looks so nice. But, to your dismay, you open the package and all that is inside is a bunch of dirty rocks. I had to ask myself if that is how I am. Do people meet me and think that I seem kind, but when they get to know me, they find out that I'm just a phony, that I'm nothing but a bunch of dirty rocks?

    There are also those who believe that if you do enough kind things you will go to heaven, and it doesn't work that way either. We are not saved because of the kind things we do, but because we are saved, we are required to do kind things. I began to realize that if I am really filled with Christ's goodness, I won't show kindness because I am required to. I will show kindness because I want to. But this can only happen if I allow the Holy Spirit to work in my life. I can't do it on my own. My own human emotions can easily take over and kindness and goodness are not evident. In fact, my human reaction to those who don't treat me right is revenge. I begin wondering how I can get back at them and make them feel as bad as I do.

    Luke 6:45 reads, "A good person produces good things from the treasury of a good heart, and an evil person produces evil things from the treasury of an evil heart. What you say flows from what is in your heart." It goes back to what we have talked about when I said that the kind of fruit, which grows on the outside, is evidence of the nature of the tree. Apples grow on apple trees and peach trees produce peaches. The fruit of the Spirit, which grows in your life, is an outgrowth of what's inside you. So if I'm not a truly good person on the inside, filled with the Holy Spirit and allowing Him to control my life, then what I produce on the outside isn't going to be very pretty.

The problem is that society is really good at filling our minds with things that aren't good. Little by little these things can infiltrate us and begin to take over our thoughts and actions. We can easily slip into the mode of just looking out for ourselves and not caring about being kind to others and being truly good. I read a disturbing article one day that said, "swearing at work boosts team spirit and morale." Wow! Who would have ever thought that swearing could help you in your job? Pretty sad, isn't it? That is the kind of influence that the world can have on our mind, and we have to be diligent in making sure we are filling our minds with thoughts that are pleasing to the Lord. It shouldn't matter what surroundings we are in or who we are with, what comes out of us should be consistently kind and good.

Image Seeker Prayer

Father, I want to be genuinely filled with Your kindness and goodness. Help me to stop demanding perfection from those I meet, instead accepting them for who they are and for whom God has made them.

Day 20
Back Surgery – Part 1

But if it were me, I would encourage you. I would try to take away your grief (Job 16:5).

The year 2000 ended up being a nightmare year in my life. On a Saturday morning in November, I reached for a glass of water on the kitchen counter and the worst pain of my life shot down my leg. The pain was so severe that it made me drop to the floor. I was alone in our home at the time, but my husband was on our property in our business office, so I crawled to the telephone and called him for help.

It turned out that I had herniated a disc in my back, causing the width of my spinal column to be a third of the size that it should have been. As a result, all of the nerves in that area were being pinched, causing the horrific pain that I was experiencing. Surgery was scheduled for the day before Thanksgiving, to clean out the area and hopefully relieve me of my pain.

The surgery was deemed a success and I was sent home the same day. We returned home that evening and when I stepped out of our automobile, the disc reherniated. Even though I thought the first round of pain that I had was as bad as it could get, I soon learned that the second time around would be even worse. Any walking sent electrical shocks through my body that were unbearable. As a result, I returned to the operating room four days before Christmas. When the surgeon opened up my back once again, I was told that he gasped. Part of my disc had literally shattered in my spinal column and was cutting into the nerves.

This surgery was a success and before long I returned to a normal schedule, thinking my back problems were in the past. But, as I prepared to walk out on the platform one Sunday in March of 2001 to lead our worship service, the disc herniated once again. This time, I told the surgeon that he might as well put a zipper in my back to make it easier to make my repairs! This third, and fortunately, final back surgery in that area was much more extensive and included rods, screws, and grafting. Recovery was not what I would call "fun," but was well worth getting my life back!

Through those days, only one Bible verse really stuck in my mind. It was Psalm 56:8, "You keep track of all my sorrows. You have collected all my tears in your bottle. You have recorded each one in your book."

For some reason, it was comforting to know that God cared enough about me during those days to collect my tears in a bottle. And believe me, He must have had a barrel to hold all of those tears that were shed and a large library to hold all of the books with my tears recorded.

Whatever you are going through today, take comfort in the fact that God sees your tears. He not only sees them, but He is collecting them. Who knows, maybe those tears will someday be used to give you showers of blessings.

Image Seeker Prayer

Father, thank You so much for comforting us during the times in life that bring tears. It is such a comfort to know that You also wept and that You designed our tears as something not to be ashamed of, but as a way to express our pain and hurt.

Day 21
Back Surgery – Part 2

God has given each of you a gift from his great variety of spiritual gifts. Use them well to serve one another (I Peter 4:10).

Why did I share my story of back surgeries with you? Was it to impart with you some theological gems that I learned from the Lord during those awful days? Nope; unfortunately it was just the opposite. I remember well-meaning friends telling me that they couldn't wait to hear everything I had learned during this time and how much closer I had grown to the Lord. I hated to disappoint them, but there wasn't much to proclaim. You see, most days during those four-and-a-half months were filled with such intense pain that my brain couldn't have grasped a children's book, let alone Scripture! We just existed during that time and survived by getting through one day at a time.

I had other friends who told me that the Lord had allowed this to happen to me, because He knew that I needed to slow down. They thought this experience was to give me rest that *they* thought I needed. I politely told them that I thought there may have been other experiences that would have given me more rest than months of excruciating pain (like maybe a vacation in Hawaii). I know that they meant well, but this

Image Seeker

explanation only made me feel guilty and punished for leading a full, busy life.

Was the Lord faithful as we went through this valley? He most certainly was. He heard every cry, every scream, and He even listened to me rant and rave when I questioned Him as to why I had to endure the pain. He didn't scold me for crying or make me feel like I had done things to cause this situation. He just held us during those days, giving us the strength to put one foot in front of the other.

That is why I am sharing this experience with you. I don't think that everything bad that happens to us in life is either a punishment for something we've done or to teach us great scriptural truths. Sometimes, the Lord allows us to travel roads that really aren't for us at all; they are to give us the wisdom to help others who may be going through similar sufferings on their journey. Even though I never felt like I gained great wisdom as a result of all the surgeries, I now have an entirely new outlook for other people who are hurting physically and who may be going through their own valley in life.

This was reaffirmed to me one day when a friend, after discovering he had a herniated disc, was facing surgery. He called and talked to me and said several times during our conversation, "I know that you understand exactly how I am feeling, LuAnn, and that really helps. Others just don't have a clue the extent of pain that I'm in." Our sharing together was a reminder to me that my experience was to be used to be a comfort to others that may be facing similar life struggles. That is why Christ came to us as a man, so that He could experience everything that we would experience. If He did that for us, can't we do it for Him?

Image Seeker Prayer

Father, thank You for Your loving arms that sustain us during the valleys of life and for the privilege of helping others as a

LuAnn Gerig Fulton

result of Your loving care. May we be willing to share Your love with those who may need our comfort and understanding instead of our scrutiny or condemnation. Help us to realize that we may be the closest image to Jesus that some people will ever see, so it is so important that our actions reflect Your love.

Day 22
The Fruit of the Spirit is Faithfulness

Never let loyalty and kindness leave you! Tie them around your neck as a reminder. Write them deep within your heart (Proverbs 3:3).

Our next attribute is faithfulness. In these times we live in with half of all marriages still ending up in divorce, with many people getting stabbed in the back in the workplace from people they thought they could initially trust, with friendships falling apart because one friend betrays another, faithfulness is becoming a forgotten quality. This characteristic is not only needed in our own personal relationship with God, but it is also needed in our personal relationships with our friends and family.

Faithfulness means to be trustworthy, dependable, and reliable. Christ is our example of true faithfulness. In Hebrews 10:23 Paul tells us, "Let us hold tightly without wavering to the hope we affirm, for God can be trusted to keep his promise." In Hebrews 11:11, Sarah shares with us how faithful she knew her God to be, "It was by faith that even Sarah was able to have a child, though she was barren and was too old. She believed that

Image Seeker

God would keep his promise." Paul and Sarah both knew that no matter what, in every situation or circumstance, their God would be faithful.

I remember when I was a child, my Mom would sometimes tell me to shut my eyes and hold out my hands. This was usually a sign that I was in for a good surprise. Now, if my older brother told me to do that, I knew to cheat and keep one eye open, because who knew what he would do to me. But I trusted my Mom; she had proved to me many times that she was faithful and trustworthy so I would automatically shut my eyes and wait with anticipation. Whatever she was going to give me, I was ready to take.

If I really possess this attribute of faithfulness, then I should also be someone who can be trusted. I should be a person who is faithful in my relationship with my spouse, my children, and my friends. Too many people are bailing out from their marriage and their family when they hit a few minor speed bumps in their journey together. Too many spouses are having affairs, destroying all of the trust and faithfulness that may have been built up in their years of marriage. If I am a truly committed Christian, there is *no* place in my life for being unfaithful.

Too often, we as Christians aren't faithful even in the little things. We can't be depended on to do what we've said we would do. We don't keep our promises; we fail to pay our bills promptly. We are late for appointments and are careless in our everyday responsibilities. As faithful, Spirit-filled Christians, we should be able to be depended upon to do what we say we will do. What kind of witness do you think we are if we are chronically late to appointments? When we tell someone we will do something, but never get around to fulfilling that promise, what message does that send to that person? When someone shares a need with us and we quickly reply, "I'll be praying for you," do we really do it? Or is that something we say to sound spiritual? You see, we are a witness to everyone that we meet, and we can either be a good witness or a bad one.

When we stand before Christ, His question to us will not be, "How much were you noticed?" Or even, "How much did you do?" Rather, I think His question will be, "Were you faithful in fulfilling your calling where I placed you?" If He has placed you as a stay-at-home mom or dad, are you faithful? If He has placed you in the workplace outside the home, are you faithful? If He has placed you in retirement, have you gotten better and stayed faithful as you have gotten older or have you gotten bitter? It doesn't matter where you have been placed, or what stage of life you are in, Christ calls us to be faithful.

Image Seeker Prayer

Father, help me to be faithful in every area of my life. Wherever You place me, give me the desire to always do what I say I will do, and help me to "ooze" goodness and kindness with everyone that I meet.

Day 23
Letting Go

I take joy in doing your will, my God, for your instructions are written on my heart (Psalm 40:8).

Through most of our middle child's high school days, she thought she would someday work in the field of music. Megan is a pianist, self-taught guitarist, and shares her love of the Lord vocally. It was just always a given that this was the field that she would explore.

But as Megan entered her senior year, her spirit became troubled. She felt the Lord was telling her that music was not to be her vocation; yet she didn't sense a strong leading into any other area. She had a passion for missions and wondered if that was where the Lord was leading her. Her youth pastor at the time knew of her struggle and invited her to go to a program at our local university where members of a missionary group would be sharing. Megan came home that day pumped and ready to send in her application to join the group.

Unfortunately, I didn't share her excitement. If she were accepted into this ministry, she would be living in the inner city of Atlanta, walking the streets by herself on a daily basis. The thought of sending my beautiful, eighteen-year-old daughter into those dangerous surroundings for a year wasn't what I envisioned for her, and I began to argue with the Lord. I wanted Him to understand that this was asking too much of her and of me to have her live and work in these precarious surroundings.

As I was struggling with all of this, my husband — in his infinite wisdom — asked me to remember what we had done with each of our children after they were born. He wanted me to think back to the times we stood in front of our church and dedicated each precious baby to the Lord. We vowed to raise them in a Christian home, nurturing them and doing our best to prepare them to serve the Lord. Dan asked me if we had put the stipulation in our vow that we would raise our children for the Lord as long as they stayed in our area where it was safe. Of course we hadn't; we had promised the Lord that we were dedicating them for His service wherever that may be.

I began to loosen my grip and allowed Megan to serve where the Lord was calling her to go. That didn't mean it was an easy year for any of us. To complete her volunteer and ministry tasks, Megan walked the inner city streets during the day, many times walking alone to and from houses in her community. She was often in dangerous situations, being mistaken on several occasions as a prostitute, for, as she puts it, "drug dealers and prostitutes were the ones populating the streets during the day." She was yelled at, followed, and propositioned; but the Lord was so faithful. In every situation, He protected her and got her to safety before she could be harmed.

The Lord not only protected her during that year, but He also blessed her abundantly for her faithfulness. She had the privilege of forming relationships with many of her neighbors as she shared God's love with them. She developed courage that amazed me as she learned to put her complete trust in her Savior. She learned the importance of being "Jesus with skin on" to many people that had never met her Lord. And she truly learned that wherever God places us, He promises to be faithful and supply all of our needs!

LuAnn Gerig Fulton

What are you holding on to that you need to loosen your grip? Are you struggling with letting your children go or allowing yourself to follow His leading? Remember that as Christians, everything we have is the Lord's to use as He desires; we are just the caregivers. What a privilege that is, and it is only when we surrender everything to the Lord and allow Him to have complete control that we can become more like Him!

Image Seeker Prayer

Father, thank You so much for allowing us to be a part of Your plan. Help us to loosen our grip on the people or things that are keeping us from surrendering to Your will, and then please hold our hand as we trust You even if we are called to unknown territory.

Day 24
I'm So Vain

For the Lord is the Spirit, and wherever the Spirit of the Lord is, there is freedom. So all of us who have had that veil removed can see and reflect the glory of the Lord. And the Lord – who is the Spirit – makes us more and more like him as we are changed into his glorious image (2 Corinthians 3:17-18).

I've never thought of myself as being a vain person. The idea of being vain makes me think of someone who thinks too highly of their appearance, status, and achievements. Nope, didn't think that was me… until recently.

I, like so many other women, color my hair. My mother had very few gray hairs at eighty, but I have not been that lucky. If I would just let my hair go natural, there would be more gray hair than any other color and I refuse to look older than I am until I have to (oops… is that a sign of vanity)?

So, on a recent evening, I decided it was time to cover up the ever-multiplying "silver" follicles (silver sounds so much more attractive than gray)! I went through my normal routine, making sure every hair was covered. I waited the allotted time and then rinsed it out. I wrapped a towel around my head and proceeded to the mirror to comb out my hair. Life was good until I took the towel off.

To say my reflection in the mirror was shocking is an understatement. I have been a blonde since I was born and I had no intention of changing that fact. But what I saw was not blonde hair; it was dark brown. My mouth dropped open, my eyes grew wide, and I suddenly felt sick to my stomach. My first thought was that maybe it would look lighter when it was dry, so I quickly grabbed my hair dryer and frantically dried my hair. Unfortunately, I was still a brunette.

Panic set in at that point and I grabbed the box of hair color that verified what I figured: I had incorrectly purchased medium brown instead of medium blonde. I rushed to the family room and told my daughter that she needed to immediately go to town and buy me the correct color. All I could think about was the fact that we had church the next day and a family gathering to go to. How was I ever going to show my face (or rather, my hair) in public? I just pictured everyone in the church gasping in horror as they saw me enter the building. I imagined fingers being pointed and snickers being heard during the service.

My daughter did as I asked and took off for town (which is twelve miles away) with a piece of paper in her hand with the kind of hair color to purchase. It wasn't long until the phone rang and she informed me that the store was completely out of my shade. So, I told her she was just going to have to go to the grocery store to get it. For the second time, the phone rang and I was given the awful news that the grocery store was also out of it. I just couldn't believe this was happening. I mean, we can put a man on the moon, but we can't keep color #8 on our shelves? They should all be ashamed of themselves!

Of course, I still wasn't ready to give up so I told Erica to go to the drug stores in town. Surely, one of them would have it. Wouldn't you know it, they were all closed for the evening. I honestly could not believe it. They were my last hope, and they were letting me down just like all the rest of the stores.

Erica returned home only to find me still ranting and raving about what in the world was I going to do? Finally, she looked at me and said, "It's only hair Mom. Get a grip!" What words of wisdom from my daughter. In the realm of life, with so many tragedies going on in our world, my being a brunette ranked pretty low. In fact, it probably didn't even register on the scale.

I went to church the next morning and to our family gathering, and do you know what I discovered? Not many people even cared what color my hair was. In fact, I'm not sure most people even knew it was a different color than before. Those that said something were told the embarrassing story and we laughed together over my error. They didn't ridicule me or shun me. It just told them what they already knew: I'm human and I'm definitely not perfect.

The ironic ending to this story is that I really like being a brunette and if I had never made this mistake, I never would have known. I don't think I would have ever been brave enough to change my hair color on purpose, so my blunder was sort of a blessing in disguise.

Since this experience, I've thought about the fact that those I meet really aren't that concerned with what color my hair is or what I am wearing. They are much more interested in knowing what is in my heart and whether I really care about them. And the more I look like Christ, the more they really won't see my exterior, because hopefully when they look at me, Christ's image will seep through.

There is no one else I would rather look like than Christ and come to think of it, He was more than likely a brunette. Oh my, sometimes Christ works in mysterious ways!

Image Seeker

Image Seeker Prayer

Father, help me to quit spending so much time worrying about my outer appearance and instead, concentrate on my inner appearance. Only then will I be a true image seeker.

Day 25
The Fruit of the Spirit is Gentleness

Let everyone see that you are considerate in all you do. Remember, the Lord is coming soon (Philippians 4:5).

Next, God also expects us to be gentle. The word *gentleness* that is found as a fruit of the Spirit reminds me of being kind and mild with other people. Unfortunately, people often take this word to mean a person who is timid or weak.

In I Timothy 6:11b Jesus said, "Pursue righteousness and a godly life, along with faith, love, perseverance, and gentleness." I Peter 3:4 says, "You should clothe yourselves instead with the beauty that comes from within, the unfading beauty of a gentle and quiet spirit, which is so precious to God." These verses show the importance that Christ places on having a gentle spirit. Nowhere in Scripture does this word carry with it the idea of weakness; instead, it compares to the taming of a highly-spirited, trained horse. The horse is anything but weak and mild. He holds his head proudly, nostrils flaring, poised to move with speed and power, but under the complete control of his master. We as Christians should be poised and ready for the race that Christ is asking us to run, full of power and the Spirit, but under His complete control.

I was thinking about a couple of examples in the Bible. Remember Peter? He was a rough and ready person until he was tamed by the Holy Spirit. Then he used all of his energy for the glory of God. Moses was an unbroken, high spirited man who needed forty years in the desert before he was fully brought under God's control. Only then was he considered to be a gentle man.

We need to remember that a river under control can be used to generate power. A fire under control can heat a home. Gentleness is power, strength, and wildness under control.

Unfortunately, not only do we often fall short in displaying gentleness to the world, we sometimes neglect or refuse to exhibit it within our own church family. There is little hope of showing the world a true example of gentleness if we haven't learned it within our church body. Ouch! That hurts, doesn't it? What happens when someone in our church family makes choices we don't approve of? How quick are we to write them off and just be thrilled and relieved that they have left the church?

Galatians 6:1 says, "Dear brothers and sisters, if another believer is overcome by some sin, you who are godly should gently and humbly help that person back onto the right path. And be careful not to fall into the same temptation yourself." According to this Scripture, how are we supposed to restore church family members who have sinned? Not only are we to restore them gently, we are to be willing to forgive them just as God has forgiven them. This doesn't mean that there is never to be discipline within the church body. In fact, and I may get flack for saying this, I don't think there is enough discipline in the church today. But in every situation, our spirit should exhibit gentleness.

"But LuAnn, you don't know how they have treated me. Why, this person has been terrible to me and talked about me. And you want me to have a part in gently restoring them?"

We can find our answer to this question in Scripture. We read in I Peter 3:15-16, "Instead, you must worship Christ as Lord of your life. And if someone asks about your Christian hope, always be ready to explain it. But do this in a gentle and respectful way. Keep your conscience clear. Then if people speak against you, they will be ashamed when they see what a good life you live because you belong to Christ." Ephesians 4:2-3 reads, "Always be humble and gentle. Be patient with each other, making allowance for each other's faults because of your love. Make every effort to keep yourselves united in the Spirit, binding yourselves together with peace."

How are we to answer those who may oppose us? Regardless of who is right in the situation, if our answer is not given with the spirit of gentleness, Christ will not be glorified. Remember, in all situations we are to be under the complete control of Jesus Christ.

Gentleness. Not an attribute that the world usually exhibits. But remember, we are not to be like the world, we are to be like Christ. And if we want to look more and more like Him, then gentleness is not an option—it's a necessity!

Image Seeker Prayer

Father, I live in a world where gentleness is not often seen or even understood. Help me to be different, filled with Your power and Spirit, and under Your complete control.

Day 26
I Stinketh!

You were cleansed from your sins when you obeyed the truth, so now you must show sincere love to each other as brothers and sisters. Love each other deeply with all your heart (I Peter 1:22).

I am an obsessive list maker. I admit it. If there was a List Makers Anonymous, I could be president. I like to start my day with a list and then love the feeling of being able to cross things off as I accomplish them. And yes, I've been known to do something not on my list and write it down and immediately cross it off, just so I have the satisfaction.

I realized one day that following a list could be disastrous. I was having a group of women to my home for supper, so my list was longer than usual. My day went well and tasks were being crossed off fairly quickly. By late afternoon, I reviewed the list and felt pretty good about my day and was happy that I even had some time left over before my guests started arriving.

Just then I happened to walk past a mirror and had an immediate, sickening realization. I had neglected to add "take shower" to my list. I guess I thought that I would just remember to do that without having to write it down. But I had been so focused all day making sure my list was conquered, that something so obvious was forgotten. I said something to Dan and he said, "You might want to shower. The ladies might think you stinketh!" Everything on my list was important, but my accomplishments might have been for naught, if the women would have been overtaken by my odor when they walked through the door.

Well, the list was completed and I managed to get a shower before the first woman arrived. We had a great night of fellowship. But it got me thinking, *How often is this scenario true in my spiritual life?* I can get so busy doing things that I think are important, making sure my agenda is accomplished (finishing a lesson plan for discipleship class or putting finishing touches on a sermon, or reading the next best book on walking with Christ), that I can sometimes neglect the obvious—taking time to call and check on a friend, writing a note to someone who is discouraged, or even slowing down long enough to smile at a frazzled cashier.

My days can become so busy doing what I would consider to be "good things" that I neglect to touch the lives of those that Christ puts in my path. I've had to ask myself if I deeply love others from my heart, or are they just an aggravating interruption to my "list."

I have come to the conclusion that Christ probably doesn't care if I have everything marked off my list at the end of the day. He is more interested in whether I took advantage of the opportunities He gave me to let others know that I care. My accomplishments may be for naught if those I meet think I stink because I don't have time for them since they weren't on my list!

Image Seeker Prayer

Lord, help me today to take my blinders off so that I can really see everyone around me. Give me Your eyes to see each person as someone You have created and who may need some of my time, even if they aren't on my list.

Day 27
Full Custody

So letting your sinful nature control your mind leads to death. But letting the Spirit control your mind leads to life and peace (Romans 8:6).

I love to read church signs. Those little pearls of wisdom such as, "YOU THINK IT'S HOT HERE? SIGNED, GOD," or "SIGN BROKEN…MESSAGE INSIDE." The signs I don't like are the ones that have the first part of the phrase on one side of the sign, and then the conclusion on the other side. That's dangerous when you are driving.

When our daughter lived in Atlanta, we drove by a church whose sign really jumped out at me. We had to drive by this church every time we went to the place we were staying, so I had the opportunity to read it many times, and I have never been able to forget it. The sign read, "GOD WANTS FULL CUSTODY…NOT JUST WEEKEND VISITATION."

I've thought about that sign many times because, unfortunately, we live in a time when we are all too familiar with what the words, "weekend visitation" mean. In a society where divorce is rampant, there are many moms and dads who know all too well the reality of only having weekend visitation with their children. Prisons are overflowing and as a result, many families face the reality of only having weekend visitation with someone they love. But honestly, if we think about it, having weekend visitation is not living in reality. If a parent is only able to see their children on weekends, that's very different than being able to care for them seven days a week, twenty-four hours a day. Visiting a family member in prison on a weekend, you can't develop the same relationship as being with them throughout the week.

Only having weekend visitation is often out of our control. Life throws us a curve ball and we can suddenly understand those words all too well. But as I've thought about this, only having weekend visitation with God is something that *is* in my control. I make the decision every day whether God will have complete control of me or if He just has some of my attention on weekends when I make my appearance at church. Do I go to church on Sundays just to get my "fix" from God for the week or am I totally surrendering to Him seven days a week, twenty-four hours a day? I'm realizing that if I really want to look more and more like my heavenly Father, I need to spend as much time with Him as I can.

The phrase "weekend visitation" made me think about the first church that we read about in the book of Acts. We are told that every day the people continued to meet together in the temple courts. They also broke bread in their homes and ate together with glad and sincere hearts, praising God and enjoying the favor of all the people. Wow! They met together every day and even ate together. They must have been so hungry to grow in their relationship with God and they knew that it would take spending time with Him and with fellow believers.

That is the kind of relationship with God that I long for — that intense, day-in-and-day-out connection with my Father where I am completely plugged into Him and His desires for my life. What is so exciting is the fact that my Father wants that same relationship with me too. The God of the universe wants to spend time with me. Why wouldn't I take advantage of that?

Image Seeker Prayer

Father, thank You so much for wanting to spend time with me so that I can look more like You. Forgive me for ever being satisfied to meet with You just on Sundays. Take control of everything I have and everything I am.

Day 28
The Fruit of the Spirit is Self-Control

A person without self-control is like a city with broken-down walls (Proverbs 25:28).

The final attribute of the fruit of the Spirit is self-control, and I don't believe that it is placed last by accident. Just like I feel that love was placed first in the fruit of the Spirit for a reason, I believe self-control was placed last for a reason. It is the fruit that makes all the rest operative. We know that controlling one's self is not possible until we surrender to Christ's management. We need to realize that we do not gain Christ through self-control; we gain self-control through Christ.

Self-control in a Christian means that instead of insisting on having our own way, we choose God's way—turning to Him for instructions and obeying His loving commands. We agree to allow the Holy Spirit to live in us and work His will through us. Then, when the Spirit has complete control of us, we can begin to look more and more like Him.

Self-control is not easy to exhibit since we all live in a very self-centered and materialistic type of world. Many people have very poor impulse control. If they see something they want, they will do anything they can to try and get it immediately. They will not be denied until they get what they are going after. It is so easy to get caught in this trap and be ruled by our flesh instead of by the Holy Spirit. Maybe you struggle with this when you are shopping. You see new clothes and you just have to have them. Maybe it is in the area of pornography, and you don't seem to have any control over what your eyes are looking at. Maybe those areas aren't any temptation to you, but in the use of your tongue, there is no self-control. I remember telling my children as they were growing up that everything that popped into their head didn't have to come out their mouth. But unfortunately, they didn't always have self-control and neither did I. We can use our tongue to do so much good in what we say, or we can use it to do so much damage in what we say to others or about others behind their back. Gossip can destroy reputations, families, and relationships. If we aren't allowing the Holy Spirit to control our tongue, there can be serious consequences.

There is something that happens in the church that can be really dangerous and that is sharing prayer concerns. Now, don't get me wrong. We should share with each other our struggles and pray for each other. That is healthy. But what isn't healthy is when someone shares with us what they are going through and then we turn around and tell someone else "in confidence." There has been more gossip done in church "in confidence" then we want to admit. So make sure if someone tells you what they are struggling with, that it stays with you and you don't share it with everyone that you meet "in confidence."

We read in James 3:8-12, "but no one can tame the tongue. It is restless and evil, full of deadly poison. Sometimes it praises our Lord and Father, and sometimes it curses those who have been made in the image of God. And so blessing and cursing come pouring out of the same mouth. Surely, my brothers and sisters, this is not right! Does a spring of water bubble out with both fresh water and bitter water? Does a fig tree produce olives, or a grapevine produce figs? No, and you can't draw fresh water from a salty spring." As I have said before, the fruit we produce is a sign of what is inside of us. And if you and I don't have God's self-control operating through us, we will have very little victory over such things as bad tempers, judgmental and critical spirits, and an unforgiving spirit.

I think self-control is often lost in the work place too. Some want a promotion so badly, that they will do anything to get one. Stepping over coworkers, ruining reputations, cutting corners, or making shady deals can sometimes seem necessary to get where we want to be. But we need to remember that God is not concerned about how far up the ladder we get, but how we lived on our journey to get there. It is so easy to get caught up in trying to get ahead, that we forget that others are watching us, and if we confess to be a Christian but aren't any different in the workplace than non-Christians, others will notice.

Self-control is a high form of worship before God. It is "living out" His commandments by doing what He asks us to do, so that He can bless us fully and trust us completely.

We have looked at love, joy, peace, patience, kindness, goodness, faithfulness, gentleness, and self-control—all attributes of the fruit of the Spirit that we are to possess. It can sometimes seem overwhelming to think about living our life, displaying each of these characteristics. But this is when we need to allow the Holy Spirit to grow the fruit of the Spirit in us. We need to surrender everything we have to God and allow Him to have complete control.

It's so easy to still be holding on to areas of our life with a tight fist and it is hindering and stifling the fruit from growing and maturing in us. Some of us may be holding on to our past. We've done things that we aren't proud of and we are stagnant because we don't think we can be forgiven. Some of us may be living in a way right now that we know isn't pleasing to God, but we haven't been willing to surrender those things to Him and allow Him to have complete control. Still, there are those of us that may be stuck living in the future. How can that happen? We are so worried about what might happen tomorrow and in the days ahead that we are frozen and paralyzed today. Only when we relinquish everything we have to Christ—our past, our present, and our future—can He begin growing His fruit within us.

Image Seeker Prayer

Father, I so desperately want to display Your attributes in my life for others to see. Work within me, so that my life will be an orchard that is full of Your fruit.

Day 29
God's Sense of Humor

For I can do everything through Christ, who gives me strength (Philippians 4:13).

Before I was married, I had certain guidelines that my future husband must measure up to for me to marry him. One was that he couldn't be more than two years older than me and secondly, my future Prince Charming couldn't be a minister (Dan fit one out of two…that isn't bad). I wasn't against ministers; I just didn't want to marry one. I grew up in a minister's home and I knew what a "fishbowl" existence that was, and I didn't want to raise a family in that setting. Plus, I had come from a very long line of ministers—a grandfather, my father, four uncles, and an aunt who was a missionary nurse in Africa. I guess I felt like my ancestors had already done our family's part in ministry, so I shouldn't have to carry it on. I enjoyed working in the church; I just didn't want to have my husband be the shepherd.

So I married Dan and we began raising our family. I'll be honest with you, when I was in the midst of those years, having three children in four and a half years, there were many times I struggled with feeling like I had no worth. I remember crying to Dan and saying that I didn't know how the Lord would ever use me in the future. I couldn't even dream at that point and think that there would be a life after children. But I remember at some point telling the Lord that I didn't know what He had in store for me, but that I wanted Him to give me the courage and strength to walk through the doors that He would open for me as He revealed His plans for my life.

The first door that opened for me was when I was asked to lead one of our worship services. My first response was, "No way. I'm not getting in front of people." Well, after searching for God's will in it, I finally said yes, and I'm here to tell you the first Sunday I did it, I thought I would have a heart attack. I was shaking and I was sure I was going to be sick. But my God proved faithful and got me through. And the more times I led, the more I enjoyed it. So then they asked, "Why don't you sing a solo some Sunday?" Once again, my response was negative, and the Lord had to work on my willingness to follow His desires. The first time I sang a solo, I not only thought I would be sick and have a heart attack, I thought I would probably wet my pants in the process!

But once I managed to make it through without any of those things happening, I thought I had probably been asked to go as far out on a limb as God would ask me to go. I had accomplished His desires and dreams for me.

Well, little did I know that He wasn't done with me yet. God began to lay on my heart such a burden for the people who were lost in our community. In fact, I would be driving down the street and as I would see people out and about, I would find myself crying, concerned that they didn't know Christ as their Savior. I couldn't figure out what was happening to me. I finally went to our pastor and told him what was going on and how I was feeling and that I thought I was losing my mind. He just sat and grinned and said, "LuAnn, it is obvious that the Lord is calling you into the ministry." At that moment, when he spoke those words, I felt like oil was being poured over my body and for the first time in a while, I had peace.

Do you get the irony in all of this? I was so adamant that I would not marry a minister, so what did God do? He called me into the ministry. What a sense of humor our God has! But notice that He didn't start out with laying on my heart that I was supposed to go into the ministry and be ordained. Why not? Because I was not ready and He knew I couldn't handle it. The entire process, starting with the day I told the Lord that I wanted Him to give me the courage and strength to walk through the doors that He would open for me, was done all in His timing. And He didn't put me into any situation until He knew I was ready.

That doesn't mean that there weren't obstacles on the journey which the Lord led me on. Let me give you a warning that you probably already know. The devil doesn't like it when we begin to take action. He is so much happier when we dwell on our excuses and we allow our fears to control us. Satan loved it when some of my first thoughts were, *What will Dan and my family think? How will I ever fit studying into my schedule to obtain my ordination?* The enemy loves it when we say we're too busy or when we say the opposite, "I've put my time in. Let the younger ones take over." By the way, I've looked through the Bible and I can't find any verse that says we are to serve the Lord only until we are seventy-two. As long as we are breathing and have the mind that God gave us, we are to be serving Him. And satan won't like that. He will put giants in your path that will seem insurmountable, and your first reaction may be to give into your fears and run. During the time that I worked on my studies, I had to have three back surgeries. I had to ask for extensions so that I could have more time to complete my work and I wanted to give up many times. The giants just seemed too big to conquer.

Completing my ordination process was, believe me, nothing short of a miracle, and I give God all the glory. Today,

Image Seeker

I can honestly say it is a privilege and an honor to be in the ministry, and I couldn't be happier to be following this dream that God has for me.

What giants are you facing today? What is God asking you to do that has you scared to death? I can guarantee you that whatever God has in store for you will be amazing and will be worth whatever obstacles you have to face. Maybe you are where I was when my children were small—so wrapped up in your daily living that you can't even figure out what your future will look like. Just be willing to give it all to God and ask Him to lead you and ask Him to show you the open doors to walk through. Because the more we follow His leading, the more we will look like Him.

Image Seeker Prayer

Father, I am so glad that You know my future and know what is best for me. Help me, Lord, to continue to walk through the doors that You open for me, even when the journey seems impossible.

Day 30
Hyper What?

After this prayer, the meeting place shook, and they were all filled with the Holy Spirit. Then they preached the word of God with boldness (Acts 4:31).

When Dan married me back in 1981, he promised to love me in sickness and in health. I am sure that vow has come back to haunt him at times since then. There was no way that any of us could have known on that day what was in store for us in the years to come.

Many times since then, specialists have looked at me and said, "Your body must be wired backward. We just don't know why it is acting the way that it is." At age twenty, I was diagnosed with a heart defect (we were just dating at the time….Dan probably should have run then when he had the chance)! One of my valves didn't seal all the way and the main nerve that led to my heart was not acting properly. Open-heart surgery was discussed, tests were run, and finally, after six long weeks, the decision was made that medication and an exercise regime would do the trick. They had no idea what caused this or why it suddenly appeared, but one year after my diagnosis, I was given a clean bill of health.

In 1983, I became pregnant with our first child and other than months of morning sickness, the nine months were fairly uneventful. That is, until her birth. For some reason, Erica didn't want to enter this world and so a long labor ensued. When she finally decided to make her entrance, she literally shot out of me and, fortunately, the doctor was there to catch her! Unfortunately, in the process, she took all of my inner muscles and nerves with her. My amazing doctor put me back together and I was ushered into my room.

A couple of hours later, I became very hot and told the nurse I wasn't feeling well. She came and checked my vitals and called for a second nurse to come. The last thing I remember is the one nurse telling the other one that she could find no pulse or blood pressure. Dan was in the hall at the time and heard the call for help in my room and for some tense moments, thought he would possibly be raising our beautiful baby girl by himself. But the Lord was gracious and allowed me to live.

At that point, I told Dan that I wasn't sure I would ever agree to have more children, but we were blessed with Megan in 1986 and Adam in 1988. Their deliveries were much more uneventful, but the pregnancies were not. With each baby, I was given bed rest for the last 4 months of my pregnancy. The babies were never in danger, but I had such severe sciatic pain in my left leg that I couldn't be upright. I also had no reflexes during the nine months. I went to several doctors and specialists and no one could figure out the reason. Everyone was puzzled as to why nothing they tried worked, but all had the same opinion. They all agreed that if I ever became pregnant again, there was a good chance I would be in a wheelchair the rest of my life. So at that point, we decided our quiver was full and our family was complete.

Following 1988, my health continued to stump the doctors. I had the three back surgeries, two bladder surgeries, one rectal surgery, and numerous times of illness that really couldn't be diagnosed. Finally, in 2008, it was found that I had another bulging disc. This time, it wasn't at the point of needing surgery yet, but I was still in great pain. They sent me to an orthopedic physical therapist to see if he could help me. Little did I know that that appointment would change my life.

After checking me over and assessing my health, he got a rather puzzled look on his face (which wasn't unusual when doctors were around me). He then told me that he felt we were dealing with more than what we thought. After doing some tests on me, he gave me a diagnosis that had eluded all the other doctors. He told me that it was obvious that I had hypermobility syndrome or some call it Ehlers–Danlos syndrome. As you can imagine, I looked at him and said, "Hyper what?" He went on to explain that in layman's terms, I have an abnormality of type I collagen. Since this collagen is responsible for helping my body hold together, it then explains why my body easily falls apart. He gave me information on this syndrome which, when we read it, sounded like an autobiography of my life.

All I could do when I received this diagnosis was cry. Not because I was upset over hearing this news, but because I finally had answers that had been sought for close to thirty years. There is no cure or treatment for this syndrome, but just having the knowledge was soothing to my soul. Finally, I knew that I wasn't imagining all the pain and disorders and that none of this had been my fault. Finally, I was armed with information that would help me in the days ahead as I learned how to better cope with this syndrome.

After this experience, I began to think about the number of people in this world that spend their entire life not searching for answers for physical ailments, but spiritual ailments. They feel lost, lonely, possibly empty inside and just like I went from doctor to doctor, they may go from person to person or get involved in one experience or another, desperate to find answers. And what saddens me the most is that I wonder how many of those people I have come in contact with but never bothered to tell them about

Image Seeker

my Jesus and about His Word. I had the answers to their searching in my possession…I could have diagnosed their "ailment" and given them the knowledge that they had long been searching for.

I think this is why it is so important that we strive to be image seekers. We need to look so much like our Jesus, that when people are around us, they just can't help but see that we are different than the world. And the more we resemble our heavenly Father, the more our actions will become like His and we won't hesitate to boldly share the good news that is in His Word.

Image Seeker Prayer

Father, thank You so much for giving me Your Word with the answers to life's questions. Give me the courage to share those answers with everyone that I meet so that they can become Your children too.

Day 31
He IS Coming Back!

However, no one knows the day or hour when these things will happen, not even the angels in heaven or the Son himself. Only the Father knows. And since you don't know when that time will come, be on guard! Stay alert (Mark 13:32-33).

Have you ever wondered what it will be like when Christ returns? I have. I know that many people have various beliefs and ideas on exactly when and how it will take place. Scripture tells us. "So you, too, must keep watch! For you don't know what day your Lord is coming" (Matthew 24:42).

I have decided to end this book by sharing with you a dream that I had one night, and I want you to know up front that the details are not supported scripturally. As most dreams are, this one was rather bizarre and strange, but it had a life-changing effect on me.

You see, I dreamed one night that we did know exactly when Christ would return. We knew the date, the hour, and even the place we needed to go to for His arrival. Each area of the country had central locations that were designated to house all Christians who were ready to meet their King at the appointed time.

Image Seeker

The location for our area was the third floor of the church that we were attending. The day arrived and people started pouring in, excitedly talking and sharing in the anticipation of Christ's return. For some reason, at some point in the dream, Christ allowed me to "float" above the room to watch everyone's arrival. I can remember experiencing such an exhilarating feeling as I saw many people whom I dearly loved enter the room.

But all of a sudden, the doors closed and the locks were turned. Those still standing outside the doors began pounding with their fists and shouting to be let into the room. I remember beginning to cry, and I told Christ that He needed to reopen the doors because not everyone was inside yet. I could see familiar faces of people that I thought for sure had accepted Christ and I was desperate to make sure they were included.

But as I pleaded, I heard the anguishing words, *Those who are pounding on the doors never accepted Me as their Lord and Savior. It is too late for them.*

I cannot explain the pain that I remember feeling at that point in the dream. It was a feeling of utter despair and agony, and at that point, I woke up in a sweat and was shaking all over.

I do not profess to be able to interpret dreams, but I believe that Christ allowed me to experience this to impress on me that everyone will experience eternity. The day will come for each of us when Christ will either welcome us into His gates to live with Him forever, or will tell us that because we did not accept Him while we were on earth, it is too late for us, and our eternity will be in hell.

This dream not only spoke to me to make sure I was ready to stand before Christ someday, but it also gave me an urgency to make sure those I come in contact with are ready to meet Him too. So I want to end this book by asking if you are ready. If your life ends today, will you be ushered into the "room" that Christ is preparing for you, or will it be too late and the doors will be locked forever? The choice is yours. I'm praying that you do not delay in your decision and accept Christ as your Lord and Savior today. You see, I can hardly wait to spend eternity in heaven, and I want to make sure that you are there with me too. And don't worry; I'll know who you are because you will look just like our Father.

Image Seeker Prayer

Father, I realize that I am a sinner and that You sent Your Son to die for me so that I can have eternal life with You. Forgive me, Father, for my sins; cleanse me and make me new. Fill me with Your Holy Spirit and give me the wisdom, power, and love to live victoriously for You until You call me home.

About the Author

LuAnn Gerig Fulton is an ordained minister who has a passion for helping others reflect Christ on a daily basis. She teaches community discipleship classes designed to give the participants a safe, loving atmosphere where they are challenged to live their lives completely dedicated to their heavenly Father. She enjoys teaching and writing, using her own life experiences as a basis for conveying biblical insights for those who desire to look like Christ. LuAnn lives in Indiana with her best friend and husband, Dan, and they have three grown children.

LuAnn would love to hear from you. You may contact her with questions, comments, or schedule her for speaking engagements on her website at: www.luannfulton.com.

More Titles by 5 Fold Media

The Purpose of Being Hidden
by Rhoda Banks
$11.00
ISBN: 978-1-936578-13-9

The Purpose of Being Hidden was written by a counselor who encounters many people struggling with these same thoughts. In this inspiring booklet, you will see that every great leader goes through their own wilderness. Joseph had to wait thirteen years before God raised him up. Even Jesus did not enter into His ministry until He was thirty years old. What if God was hiding you for a season to prepare you to be a leader and to walk in your destiny? The author's insight will give you a fresh perspective on your life and encourage you to hold on to the faith and patience required to come out as a leader on the other side.

Tour of the Tribes
by Sonny Rudd
$15.00
ISBN: 978-1-936578-07-8

The tribes, their lineage and appointed leaders were crucial in biblical times, but how does that affect us today? Whether you are new to the Scriptures or have studied them for years, *Tour of the Tribes* will help connect the dots of Bible history and lay a firm foundation for your spiritual journey.

Pastor Sonny Rudd breaks down the tribes of Israel, their key players, and how ultimately, their development all stands to represent our journey and growth in Christ. His use of Scripture, history, and personal stories clearly demonstrate God's sovereign plan for our lives in every season.

Visit www.5foldmedia.com to sign up for 5 Fold Media's FREE email update. You will get notices of our new releases, sales, and special events such as book signings and media conferences.

5 Fold Media, LLC is a Christ-centered media company. Our desire is to produce lasting fruit in writing, music, art, and creative gifts.

"To Establish and Reveal"
For more information visit:
www.5foldmedia.com

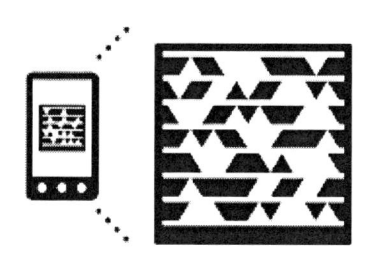

Use your mobile device to scan the tag above and visit our website. Get the free app: http://gettag.mobi

CPSIA information can be obtained at www.ICGtesting.com
Printed in the USA
LVOW102008120212

268299LV00001B/4/P

9 781936 578269